THE
CROSS
OF
CHRIST

And a Meditation

on the Seven Last Words from the Cross

By William A. Buege

CONCORDIA PUBLISHING HOUSE · SAINT LOUIS

CONTENTS

THE CROSS OF CHRIST
My Obedience to God

Luke 22:41-46
interpreted by
Phil. 2:8

"In the Cross of Christ I glory!" What a tremendous hymn, and what a stirring experience to be part of a group that is still willing to sing it with such gusto that you are convinced they mean it! What an insight to see these few words as the very heart and center of our Christian faith and to insist that this Cross, intended by the devil and his world to be the final wrecking of God's dream for man and man's final hope before God, that this itself should now tower o'er the wrecks of time, the wrecks of all the plans and ideas and proposals that over the years have set themselves in opposition to it! What an honor to live in a city whose sky is studded with crosses! What a privilege to be able to meet regularly at the foot of the Cross and through it find our real worship of God! What a holy distinction to take our little gold crosses, fasten them to our lapels, and thereby designate ourselves plainly as soldiers of the Cross! Yes, most assuredly: "In the Cross of Christ I glory!"

But is it really all that simple? Is it really in the Cross of Christ that people glory, or is it merely in some reasonable facsimile thereof? Is it truly through the Cross of Christ that we worship, or is our approach to God as slick and as sleek as those representations of the Cross which by their beauty can help us ignore as much as they can help us remember what is involved in the Cross of Christ and glorying in it? Is putting a little pin on some garment enlistment in the army of the Cross and the equivalent of unqualified loyalty to the Christ of the Cross? We need to remember that the greatest crimes have been committed not only against the Cross but also in the name of the Cross and as an expression of loyalty to the Cross. We need only remind ourselves that by bending the ends of the Cross you have a swastika, and this crooked cross apparently has followers today who use it to strike terror into people's hearts. We need only remember that the wearing of a cross is at least somewhat fashionable, fashionable enough so that the jewelers have been able to market it at a profit. We need only remember that wearers of crosses can be seen almost everywhere where people assemble. To show how little effect the cross has as cross, associated, as Christ Himself associates it, with self-denial, you will find it in places that cater specifically to self-indulgence. You will even find a cross in some instances (Heaven forbid!) on top of TV sets that do more to dull man over against God and chain man away from the worship of God than almost any device the devil has been able to lay his hands on.

Remember that the hymn asserts for us, "In the Cross of *Christ* I glory!" This is the direct opposite not only of every human inclination but also contrary to every human evaluation. Where this is truly the case, there has been some prior smashing by God, some re-molding by God of our ordinary human expectations, some leveling by God of our regular human pride, some destroying by God of our very basic human selfishness. The Cross of Christ can never be popular because it declares more forcibly than any other medium the direct opposite of the popular expectations with regard to God. It is still the stumbling block for everything in us that is

6

merit before God. It is still utter foolishness to our natural wisdom, which cannot but fashion its own image of God as well as its own expectations of God. The heart of the matter is that the Cross tells us something about God that utterly negates (i. e., crosses out) everything that is the product of our own efforts and everything that is the evaluating of our own thinking. The Cross of Christ shows us what we really accomplish when we attempt to come to God on our own terms: what then does it say of what we do when we deliberately run away from God and cut counter to His will? The Cross of Christ shows us where we really are over against God, because it reveals the depths to which God had to go in order to find us.

It is in that Cross that we say we glory, which means that we have come to bow under the verdict of God which smashes all our own verdicts. We have come to worship the God who is not God at all in man's sense of the word because He is not a God in whom you can glory as man understands glory, impressive display and overwhelming might. We kneel here before that God of whom on human terms we must be ashamed, the God whom we think we have to defend, the God whom we more often stick in the corner of our lives than display as the glory of our lives. And this shows what kind of a God He is. We get away with it. We sing our songs of allegiance here, and we declare our oaths of loyalty in these friendly surroundings, and we put on our pins which are to demonstrate our sincere attachment, and who ever hears from our lips about the Crucified, who is Jesus Christ? And who sees in our lives anything resembling an expression that shows that the Cross of Christ has become our Cross? And we get away with it! We insist that that is our glorying in the Cross of Christ,

7

and we give people an additional reason to sneer, at least in private, at this One, whom we claim as our God, and we encourage others to this same kind of glorying, which is still a glorying in ourselves. And we get away with it, because the Cross is still the Cross of Christ, His burden and His shame, because this is the kind of a world that it is and also because His are the kind of people that they are, still very much in need of His Cross!

Our prayer to this God of the Cross is that He would use this Lenten season to be just that to us: the God of the Cross, our God indeed with all that that implies, but God in and through the Cross. May He use our services here and our sermons to that end, as we attempt with His help to develop the overall theme "In the Cross of Christ I Glory." We would see only the Cross of Christ by seeing it always as His mighty deed of accomplishment for us. May He bless us to His ends this evening as we consider:

The Cross of Christ My Obedience to God

It should be noted that while Christ's Cross is that specific instrument of wood by which the Son of God was most shamefully put to death, it also denotes everything that contributed in any way to His shame and His suffering and His death. Thus in a very specific sense the summary we read to you from the lectern is a description of the Cross of Christ because it is the history of His great Passion. But there is a very real sense in which the Cross not only threw its shadow over His whole life but was also expressed in every part of it. There really is nothing of Christ's life that can be separated from the Cross. Surely we don't have to look too hard to see that the wood of the manger is part and

8

parcel of the same tree, the swaddling clothes the very closest step that there can be to the dice game over His seamless robe on Calvary, and the hard, coarse straw the most that His tender baby skin could stand until it was readied for the crown of thorns. You can tell, without being a prophet, that the religion of His day is not going to put itself out for Him but will rather put Him out as you hear the great knowers of the Scriptures tell Herod where the Child was to be born but take no step in that direction themselves. You can hardly escape the conclusion that some day their forces would catch up with Him because God would send no more angels to warn people in dreams and there would be no Egypt to which He could flee, because you can't keep running all your life. Even in His highest moments, certainly highest according to our view of the matter, the Cross was not absent. With a great deal of effort we climb a mountain with Him, but it is worth every bit of effort on our part because we finally see what we hunger to see in our Savior and our God. He is transfigured before our eyes, and the glory streaming from Him tells us plainly who He is in the very core of His Being. And when Moses and Elijah appear with Him, it is almost too much, and we want nothing more than Peter, who speaks for us when He offers to make this a shrine where we and all men can come to see what kind of Leader we really have and that we are not quite so foolish as men really pretend. But when we talk that way, we just don't know what we are saying, and we don't know what we are saying because even in the presence of God we are more ready to speak than to hear. But listen to the subject of conversation between the Christ and these two great representatives of God. They discussed the death that He should accomplish at Jerusalem. We don't even see

9

the Transfiguration aright if we see it apart from His Cross, and Moses and Elijah are witnesses that it is so.

In a sense this really dashes our hopes, just as surely as it dashed Judas' hopes. Here was a man who followed Jesus because of a grand dream and a high expectation. But when he saw how it really was, he knew that his dream was only a dream and his expectations couldn't possibly be fulfilled in following this Jesus. Jesus just wasn't the kind of Messiah and Savior that Judas had hoped, and it was the certainty of the Cross that finally brought that home to him. So Judas not only quit Christ's cause but also betrayed Christ and His cause. Let him that has ears really hear! The Cross is not only integral to the life of Christ, but it is also the heart of man's disappointment in Christ, and when men become disappointed with Christ, they not only quit His cause but betray His cause. They always hope to get something out of it that fits their expectations of what it means to have a god. What is the sense of being involved in a cause if it does not pay off? They are always still their disobedient selves, and now we are speaking fairly close to home, because far from letting God be God simply and only because He truly is God, they would dictate the terms on which they let Him be God, and they would prescribe what He must do for them if He is to be their God. And the Cross has no place in any of it, so that as soon as the Cross becomes real with its implications for them and their God, they not only beg off for themselves but also betray. "Friend, wherefore art thou come? Friend, betrayest thou the Son of man with a kiss?" To this day Christ is betrayed into the hands of the enemy more by kisses than by curses, more by shows of friendship than by open enmity, more by tokens of what should be love than by what are manifes-

10

tations of hate. I have yet to hear a church member shout out in the world that he hates Christ: but how many by their church membership are betraying Jesus, putting Christ right into the hands of the enemies, because their church membership is nothing more than a Judas kiss!

But how came the Cross to be in Christ's life, so that from beginning to end His life is nothing but a kind of crucifixion until finally the nails are driven through His hands and His feet and what always lurked there in the shadows becomes a final fact? If we answer wrong here, we have missed the real meaning of Christ's Cross, and we can miss it in two ways at least. One is that we fail to see Him aright, and the other is that we fail to see our personal involvement. There is the same dreary potential in us that there was in all the disciples, and this is how we miss so much of what God would reveal to us in Christ. In the Garden of Gethsemane they fell asleep in spite of the strongest possible warnings from Jesus Himself that they watch and pray, or they would fall into temptation. Well, they didn't watch and pray, and so they fell into temptation, the very common temptation of falling asleep, or being where Jesus was but not being awake to what He was doing, of being only a stone's throw from His agony in prayer but really being in another world because they had no part in the prayer. It is significant — what isn't when our Lord speaks to us and particularly as He takes time to speak to us out of His Great Passion? — that in these matters Jesus should point us to the single possibility open to us for a proper participation in His suffering and death: "Watch therefore and pray . . . the spirit indeed is willing, but the flesh is weak." That our spirit is willing is amply demonstrated by our being here at all. This is the last thing

11

that our flesh would bring us to do on these Wednesday nights. But when we come here even under the prompting of our spirit and in opposition to our fondest desires, we bring our flesh with us, and unless we watch we are going to fall asleep to all that Christ is here doing for us, and unless we pray we are going to lose our part in it.

With eager minds, made eager by the promise of our Lord, and with prayerful hearts, made prayerful by the indwelling Christ, who alone can bring us to pray properly, we find ourselves in Gethsemane, that heart of the mystery of the Cross but also the unveiling of the heart of Jesus, which made the Cross a reality. When we look at the Christ of the garden, we hardly recognize Him, even before His brow becomes all discolored by His bloody sweat, even before His garments testify to what He has been going through as He groveled in the dust as a worm and no man. If there is any one thing that characterized the life of Jesus, it was eagerness to do His Father's will and to finish His work. Crossing over the brook Kidron, He crossed over the final threshold that lay between Him and what He so eagerly looked forward to. But now the eagerness departs, and instead we have to hear Him tell us, "My soul is exceedingly sorrowful, even unto death." What could that mean except that something so laid hold of Him that it all but killed Him on the spot? What was it? Surely not merely the prospect of suffering; He had been the closest Friend of personal suffering all His life. Surely not merely the prospect of death, cruel and horrible as it surely was; far lesser men than He had faced the same kind of death without all but dying at the simple prospect. Here is where we are liable to miss because we do not see ourselves involved. The sorrow unto death that drove Him to His agonizing prayer, a praying such as there never

12

was before or after, was the cup about which He prayed. Upon entering the garden the cup had come so close that He could see it. He saw it held out to Him, and that by His own Father. Should He drink it or not?

"Lo, I am come to do Thy will, O My God!" That stands forever as the great theme of His whole life. Now we see Him wrestling with that will of God until His sweat falls to the ground in great drops of blood. Again and again He throws Himself on the ground to pray the same thing: "O My Father, if Thou be willing, let this cup pass from Me. Nevertheless not My will but Thine be done!" And there was no word from God, no word whatsoever. An angel comes and strengthens Him, but this only increases the agony of His praying. Obviously the angel only could help Him to face the cup, sustain His strength at least this much that He would not die before He drank it. The all-important question for us is: "What was the cup about which He prayed, pleading even from the very depths of His Being so that His self-giving in this praying even involved His blood, pleading as no one ever pleaded with God before, that if at all possible this cup might pass from Him without His drinking it? What was the cup?" It was the most horrible that could possibly happen to Him, the one thing above and beyond everything else that He did not want, and did not want with His whole Being. What could that be? Remember how calmly He had spoken of His Cross, even the bitterness of all that went before the Cross, the mockery and the spitting and the rejection? His disciples were greatly disturbed by His words, but He only set His face like flint to go to that Jerusalem of Cross and sorrow and anguish. What entered the picture so that He couldn't remain calm about it now?

Was it one thing to view it from afar and something quite different to see it now at hand?

No, it never was anything abstract or merely theoretical to Him, as so many things at a distance are to us. He lived with the reality of it all, as we pointed out before, in everything that He ever said and did. The new, the element that He couldn't possibly calculate in advance, was our sin, so becoming one with our sin that its very guilt should rest upon Him. This is what was meant by drinking the cup. This was what was so horrible and repulsive to Him, this becoming personally identified with our sin as though it were literally His own. It would mean that separation from God which sin always creates. It would mean that He could cry to God and there would be no hearing by God because God has no ear for sinners. It would mean that God's hand would be turned against Him and He would deserve it. God would look with utter revulsion at Him without any of that good pleasure of God resting upon Him that was the very heart of His life and the bread of His days. It meant fully taking our place, being before God and men what we really are, and so taking everything that we had deserved. Look at me! Am I so bad? And Jesus sweat blood praying not to be completely identified with me before God!

But He drank the cup. He established the identity. It was the Father's will. So when He rose up from praying He saw Himself as I am, because He went and did what He did for me. He knew that God saw Him as God sees me, and that was the great hurt that He could hardly stand, the great hurt that almost killed Him before they hung Him on the Cross. They hung Him on the Cross? Now I see how I hung Him there because

14

in drinking the cup He established identity with me. Something like Dr. Jekyll and Mr. Hyde: Christ drinks and God's Jekyll becomes Buege's Hyde, so that is all that God sees now when He looks at His own Son. Now we see also that this was not thrust upon Him as something that He could not avoid. This was not His fate as it is our fate. He drank the cup willingly because it was the Father's will. Or as St. Paul says it, He humbled Himself and became obedient unto death, even the death of the Cross.

I never was obedient to God, neither in the little nor in the great things of life. I really never even bothered to ask what God wanted, or if I did, I never really lived it that way. Or if it looked as if I did, my heart wasn't in it, and I resented the will of God as it was opposed to my will. I have no obedience of my own to offer God. If I had, it wouldn't have been quite so bad for Jesus to make the identity with me absolute. But He did drink the cup, and now I no longer see myself by myself. Now I look and see Jesus for me, every step my step, every hurt my hurt, every drop of blood my blood flowing from me, every moment in hell my eternity of hell. But never forget that He did it. He drank the cup to its bitterest likeness to me and oneness with me, did it because it was the Father's will. He became obedient unto death, even the death of the Cross. Here then was something else. Surely He was obedient to God from all eternity because He and the Father were One and Their wills coincided perfectly. But now He *became* obedient in this new way, this obedience which involved the Cross. This was something different, and the different was that it was *for me,* the becoming obedient was the becoming obedient for me. Now I go to Sinai with its demands upon me which I do not fulfill and with its sore threats

15

upon me for not fulfilling, but I do not go on my own, or I would die if I ever touched the Holy Mount. I now offer perfect obedience to every demand there made, which means to every demand of the holiness of God. The great "Thou shalts" and the "Thou shalt nots" thunder at me as loud as ever, but I can insist that they cannot possibly frighten me any longer. I point them to Jesus Christ who humbled Himself and became obedient for me, obedient for me even unto death, yes, the death of the Cross. Sinai, hear! God of the Law, listen to what is prayed in the bloody sweat of Gethsemane: "Father, not My will but Thine be done." That, heavenly Father, is the only obedience which I even attempt to offer, because I believe that it is full obedience for me. Amen.

THE CROSS OF CHRIST
My Innocence Before God

Matt. 26:66
in the light of
Rom. 3:19

"In the Cross of Christ I glory," we sing, and if we have any idea at all of what we are singing, we must surely know that there is something heroic about such a glorying. It puts us into the noble company of Paul, who could look over mighty Rome with all its very evident power and confront it all with the Cross of Christ because he was not ashamed of the Gospel. It identifies us as being in the grand tradition of Stephen, who kept insisting on what is the glory of the Cross until the stones stilled his testimony and he was received by the Lord of the Cross standing at the entrance of the open heavens to welcome one who had gloried in His Cross so fully and so nobly. It reveals us to one another, but no longer by hidden and surreptitious signs hastily drawn in the dust and just as hastily erased because of the awful possibility of the Cross becoming the instrument of the confessor's death: now it shows us openly to one another so that we are not only people who meet under the Cross, not only people for whom the Cross means very much, but actually people who share a common boast and hold out a united witness, the Cross of Christ as the only glory they would be known by, the only standing that they seek before God and men.

But perhaps, when we begin to give it such a personal twist, we are not so sure that the Cross of Christ is so fully all that to us. The company of Paul, yes, because

17

that is indefinite enough not to call for any personal commitment; the noble army of martyrs, yes, because at present there is no power arraigned against us that would make us put our blood where our mouth is; membership in a congregation that exalts the Cross and a Synod that insists that the Cross is central, yes, because that is still far enough removed from daily life to make it just another expression in addition to our other expressions, an expression that we regard as having religious meaning only with its meaning disassociated from our days. We don't want to go overboard on this sort of thing as though there were nothing else in life and as though there were nothing else to judge life by and to face life with and to interpret life under. If to glory in the Cross means to glory in it so exclusively that you don't glory in anything else except as it exalts the Cross, then we are not so sure, and we would not want to say unequivocally that this is what we mean when we sing our hymn. Certainly this is not what we mean when we pin a gold cross on our lapel. We can readily see that this should tie up with the great cross and its meaning here at church, but that it should be as central to our lives as the great Cross is to our church so that nothing is done except as it is done under the Cross, and nothing is seen except in view of the Cross, and nothing is contemplated except by considering the Cross — well, that is something else, and we would be hypocrites if we said anything more.

And yet how else can we glory in the Cross of Christ except as we glory in nothing else besides? It still stands on the basis of no less than Christ's own word: "You cannot serve two masters, for either you will love the one and hate the other, or else you will cling to the one and despise the other." For all of our modern effort in that direction, "ye cannot serve God and mammon!" If the Cross of

18

Christ is not central to everything, then it must stand alongside something else. If the Cross of Christ does not interpret everything for us, then some things interpret the Cross for us. Actually, to glory in the Cross of Christ means that we make it play second fiddle to nothing, that no meaning apart from it itself will give meaning to us, that far from sticking it off into some forgotten corner of our lives we plant it out there where men recognize it as our boldest claim. If I glory in the Cross of Christ, then the Cross of Christ is my glory, and I cannot be understood apart from it because without it my life has no glory. It has gone dead and flat just as surely as a light bulb that gives no light, just as surely as salt that has lost its savor and is good for nothing but to be cast out on the ground and to be trodden underfoot.

Genuine glorying in the cross means that there has been a rearrangement of life, so much so that it really isn't the same life any more that it once was. All the things in which we once naturally gloried because they are so glorious in themselves and have such attractiveness for us, have lost their charm for us or are resisted in their attempt to charm us. This isn't a mere changing of our minds as we change our minds in a choice of hats; this isn't a simple growth by which our tastes no longer are what they once were: This is nothing less radical than conversion, a complete about-face from what we once were, nothing less than personal death by which we die to what we once were and rise again to newness of life. This is the meaning of that paradox by which Paul interpreted his own life for anyone who is interested in being like him: "I live, yet not I, but Christ liveth in me, and the life which I now live in the flesh I live by the faith of the Son of God, who loved me and gave Himself for me." Without this, our glorying is not good, though we insist that it is a glorying in the Cross. Without this we are merely using the right words on the right occasion and will change the words when the occasion demands other words. We pray God for the change that is nothing less than regeneration, rebirth, change in the very root and fiber of our being, by bringing us to see the Cross in His light, which means our involvement in it. May God bless us this evening as we consider:

The Cross of Christ My Innocence Before God

If we are to glory in the Cross of Christ, then it goes without saying that it must mean to us what God intended it to mean. That it was something that God wanted Christ to endure is written deep into the whole meaning of the Gospel. As horrible as it was, it was the goal which God set for Christ in order that He might be the Savior of men; it was the altar that God Himself erected in order that His Christ might be His true Lamb to take away the sins of the world. That it involved far more than we can possibly picture for ourselves is readily seen as we watch our Savior agonize in prayer in the Garden of Gethsemane. That it was the will of God and apart from it there could be no obedience to God is amply shown by the fact that though God's own Son cried out with tears and agony and strong groanings, the conclusion of it all was not that it was taken away but the firm resolve: "Arise, let us be going. Behold, he is at hand that doth betray Me!" It may be that there is one aspect to Christ's Cross that we often overlook and thereby deprive ourselves of both additional insight into what it was and also stronger faith that it was for us: We fail to consider the devil's attitude toward the Cross. If we would attempt to assess this on our own, we would immediately think that the devil erected the Cross, that

20

it was the one place where he wanted his Archenemy to end up so that He would be totally discredited and just as defeated by that tree as Adam and Eve were by the tree in the garden. This, however, is not the case but is an evaluation which basically holds that the Cross was merely something hurtful and harmful to Jesus, that it merely shows what happens to particularly holy people, that it does nothing more than represent in intensified form the ongoing battle between good and evil, with good always coming out second best because this is the kind of a world that it is.

However, on at least two occasions, the Scriptures vividly portray Satan's opposition to the Cross, such opposition that it was literally the last thing that he wanted, His very cunning approach to Jesus with the suggestion that Jesus jump off the pinnacle of the temple because God would give His angels charge over Him was the most flagrant temptation to bypass the Cross. It suggested display, sensationalism, eye-catching advertisement for which human eyes are always so hungry, all this as being the way of gaining a following; not the Cross where it will be only too evident that God's angels are not attending You, where men will cry out with perfect human logic, "If Thou be the Son of God, come down from the Cross!" It was exactly the same effort of the devil that put such groanings into the praying of Gethsemane, to bypass the will of God because doing God's will came too dear, God's will demanded far too much. Jesus fought off this temptation by refusing to tempt the Lord, His God. Not to do God's will even though it means the Cross, is nothing less than blasphemy, tempting God, putting Him on the same level with the devil.

The other occasion when the devil plainly showed his

21

own concern with the Cross and his never-ending attempt to prevent the Cross came at one of the high moments of Jesus' life, and God knows, according to our way of seeing things, there were none too many of them. Peter had just finished with his grand confession of faith that Jesus was the Christ the Son of the living God, and Jesus was grateful that His Father had been able to use His efforts to bring about this kind of saving faith. So Jesus attempted to lead His disciples deeper into the mysteries of His Being and the purpose of His coming as the Christ. He told them how from that moment on His life would be a going up to Jerusalem, where He would be mocked and spitefully entreated and spit upon and put to death by the Gentiles. And here is what we come to only too often, the Peter of the grand confession still did not fully know what he had said because now he insisted that this should be far from Christ. If flesh and blood had not revealed to Peter that Jesus was the Son of God but the Father in heaven had opened his heart for that marvelous confession of faith, then we merely have further evidence that where God is at work He is never at work alone. Where God builds His church, there the devil always erects his chapel, and the Peter of the grand confession was seen by Jesus as an instrument of Satan. Not go up to Jerusalem, however well intentioned by Peter this suggestion might have been? "Get thee behind Me, Satan, for thou savorest not the things of God but the things of men." It was the regular tried and trusted method of the devil to get Jesus to do things man's way because He was a man, and that would mean not doing them God's way because man has no taste for the things of God.

Why did the devil try so desperately to keep Jesus from the Cross? Because it was the battleground where the devil's power over man would be broken. Up to the Cross

the devil had a real claim on us, by our personal rejection
of God and our choice of the devil and by God's own
justice, which could make no other response to our action
than to declare us guilty, guilty of rebellion, guilty of despising God, guilty of cutting ourselves off from Him by
whom alone we have life. God is just, and since we had
chosen evil, God had no recourse but to give us over to
the evil because He couldn't possibly ignore it. We belong
to him whom we obey, and since we had obeyed the devil
and not God, we openly insisted for earth and heaven and
hell to hear that by this obedience we were declaring ourselves free from God and giving ourselves over to the
claims of the Evil One. "Choose you this day whom you
will serve!" This was the demand which confronted us
every day of our lives. "If the Lord be God, then serve
Him." But we did not serve Him and thereby insisted
that He was not the Lord, our God. And so God, who
would not hold us by force, had to give us up to whatever
we would have for ourselves. He had no choice but to
give us up. He is the Father who warned and pleaded
and rebuked and threatened, but all to no avail. Like the
Prodigal, who could no longer stand the cramped quarters
of his father's house, we took what our Father had given
to us and wasted it in a far country, away from our Father,
away from His restrictions, away from any claim which
He might still make upon us. You can call the far country
by whatever name you will, it is not the Father's house,
the Father's love and discipline. It is being away from
God, and that means belonging to the devil.

Now the devil did not want Christ to go to the Cross,
because this would open to men the possibility of return
to God. How so? This is where we need all the insight
which God Himself can give us so that we see the Cross
under the light which He sheds upon it, for only so will

23

we see the Cross in relation to ourselves. The last desperate hope of the devil today is that we do not read God's meaning in the Cross, that all this that Jesus endured be regarded by us as some history which He had to live through, or what is even worse, that we see it merely as something which some very mean and wicked people did to this very best of men. Then the whole thing lends itself very well to dramatization but hardly to personal application. Then we can be moved by it so that we can even find some tears spilling over, at least in our hearts if not in our eyes, but we will in no way glory in it as being the achievement of the Son of God for us. The question of the old Negro spiritual is still pertinent. "Were you there when they crucified my Lord?" But it isn't enough. We are not merely to be there in the sense that we see everything that is given to us to see; we are to be participants, and there is no part from which we are left out.

If we don't learn this anywhere else, we surely must learn it from Peter. When the soldiers bound Jesus and led Him away to the High Priest, we read that then all His disciples forsook Jesus and fled, even Peter. But why *even* Peter? Surely we don't expect him to be some kind of superman who would be so very much different than the rest of the disciples. No, we don't think that he was a superman, but he himself had thought that he was one. Jesus had warned him that he with all the rest would be offended because of Him that very night. We don't hear too much from the rest of the disciples, but Peter protested loud and long that he would never be offended in Jesus, even though he should die with Jesus. It wouldn't take much change in Peter's words to make them come out like a long and loud and rather glamorous protest that we made in exactly the same area and to the same end. Remember your confirmation? How you insisted

24

before all who would listen that you would remain faithful to this Christ even unto death? Peter was also warned that though his intention was very good, his flesh was still weak, and the only way that he could offset its influence was to watch and to pray. But Peter did not watch and pray, and so he fell into temptation, exactly the same as we fall into the same temptation, not merely going to sleep now, although that is part of it, but actually denying Jesus; insisting so loudly and so convincingly that we don't know Him that finally others take us at our word and regard us as people who don't even know Jesus.

What was behind all this? Well, Peter, who had run away, no doubt figured that he had made quite a fool of himself in the running, had certainly given the lie to the very bold protest that he had made to Jesus' warning. So he headed back to where Jesus had been taken bound. What did he intend to do there? Confess Christ? Throw himself between Christ and His accusers and let himself be killed as evidence against everything that they claimed of Christ? The Scriptures tell us that he followed afar off to see what the end would be. He merely wanted to be an onlooker, which means that he really did not want to get involved. Except that here is one place where you are never merely an onlooker. You are involved, either on the side of Jesus or on the side of His accusers; either witnessing for Christ by insisting that you have no other life and you will really die before you give Him up or by denying Christ as Peter did and then having Jesus turn and look upon you so that if He still has any meaning at all for you, you go out and weep bitterly. What was Peter really saying here when he cursed and swore that he did not even know the Man? He was denying what he had so bravely confessed when he had declared that Jesus was the Christ, the Son of the living God. He was insisting:

25

"Whatever I might have claimed once, I don't claim it any more. I was deceived so much that from what I see here I now must swear to you that I don't really even know this Man. I take an oath before God on it." And what did that really mean? It meant that Peter was saying that Jesus should be put to death.

This is nothing more or less than what we claim, claim just as loudly as Peter did with every sin that we have ever committed, especially we who no longer can sin apart from the Cross because we have sung that it is in the Cross of Christ that we glory. By our sin we disown Jesus as the Son of God, our Savior. By our sin, we insist that He has saved us from nothing. By our sin we tell all who see it or hear it that we do not know this Man and under no circumstance is anyone to regard Him as our Lord, as the One who alone has the right to tell us what to do. And so we stand there with Peter to back up the Sanhedrin, which always represents the highest to which religion can attain when it is our own best product, and insist that this Jesus is guilty of death. But there is also a deeper sense in which we so insist, and that is in humble penitence, genuine sorrow, which is made soul-sorrow by God Himself when we see Jesus standing there for us. Every mouth is stopped in that all are guilty before God. Jesus is here declared guilty as I confess that I have sinned and come short of the glory of God.

This is the court of God that is being held here, because the High Priest, for all his abuse of his office, still acted on God's behalf. But if we are going to see God behind the High Priest, then we need to refocus so that we see ourselves standing before God's tribunal instead of Jesus standing there. This is the only way in which it makes sense to declare that Jesus is guilty, death guilty.

26

"What think ye?" God asks of all His holy commandments. "What accusations do you bring?" And we haven't a protest to make. We haven't a shred of innocence that we can offer the holiness of God. Guilty, guilty of death, the death that is eternal hell. That court has already been held because Jesus stood for me before the High Priest's court. God was there behind the High Priest, unless we have already forgotten that Jesus sweat blood in Gethsemane as He prayed that God's will might be done. And I was there before God because Jesus had declared under oath that He was truly the Son of the living God. That is what made Him guilty, my awful guilt. That's what shaped His Cross and brought Him to hell: He was guilty because He had really drunk the cup; He was guilty because He stood there fully in my place; He was guilty as hell itself is guilty because He was guilty with my guilt. And so everyone and everything combined in the sentence upon Him, even God, yes, especially God: "He is guilty of death!" And so they lead Him off to the death of which He was guilty because of my guilt. But look, here I still stand before God, the God of judgment, the God of the commandments of accusation and the commandments of demand, demand for nothing less than perfect innocence. Now I can stand there because Jesus went off guilty of death with my guilt. So the Cross of Christ, the guilt of Christ, the death of Christ, means the end of my guilt. It means nothing less than my innocence before God, my perfect innocence in the Christ who became guilty with my guilt. Amen.

THE CROSS OF CHRIST
My Power from God

> *John 18:36, 37*
> *in the light of*
> *1 Cor. 1:18*

If we were to summon all the faith that God has ever
created in us, and if it were the most fundamental trust
and confidence of our lives, and if we were to express
it all in a single prayer that would plead with God Himself to break into our days and prevent that which we
regard as our most dangerous temptation, the sin which
most sorely besets us, where would we begin? Suppose it
would be within our power to summon the Almighty
Himself to clear the way that still lies before us of
everything that we are sure should not be there — to what
ends would we summon God? What would we have Him
do at our special bidding? Let us say that, instead of
being only a somewhat meaningless expression, what we
would then ask to be forbidden would never again rise
up to plague us — what would follow? God forbid that
I should linger in devastating illness, illness that would
lay its deadly hand upon me without killing me, without
stopping my heart, until it had stopped every other func-
tion that has meaning! God forbid that my home should
ever be laid waste as I have seen so many homes laid
waste, that my family should be scattered to the four
winds with no attachment of love remaining, with no
cords of concern binding at least their hearts to one
another! God forbid that I should ever again be as close
to those powers of wholesale destruction as I once was!
God forbid that wicked and cruel men should be able

28

to unleash the threat which today holds all thinking people in fear and forebodes the bitterest kind of future for our children if it be any kind of a future at all! God forbid — but why continue when each of us could multiply almost endlessly what each wants God to keep from him or to keep him from, when each of us would only need to reveal the content of his daily prayers to reveal what we most dearly want God to forbid?

But for all the sincere trust that our praying shows and for all the genuine concern for our poor world that our praying demonstrates, how many of us would be as willing to pray just as eagerly that God forbid for us what Paul asks God to forbid in his life? Here it is, and it was Paul's personal summons of the Almighty to step in and actually forbid — what? God forbid that I should glory save in the Cross of our Lord Jesus Christ! If we had to attempt to paraphrase that, it would sound something like this: God, Thou knowest the weakness of my nature, my easy slipping away from Thee and the things that are Thine, my seeking of my own and the things that are mine, my being attracted all but irresistibly to the old patterns and the habitual ways of looking at things; most mercifully step in and prevent it all, so that I may never glory in anything that does not represent a glorying in the Cross of Jesus Christ, that I may never desire or boast of anything that will take the Cross out of the center of my life or deprive it of its meaning for my life. And we remember in faith that praying is not saying something that we regard as acceptable, not going through some form merely that is religiously oriented so that it is a recognition of our duty and responsibility over against God. Prayer is the most fervent expression of trust that God will do as we ask Him. Therefore if we pray that God forbid our glorying

29

in anything save the Cross of Christ, we can fully expect God to intervene in all of our affairs in such a way that the Cross of Christ be to us all that God ever intended. Prayer being what it is, that is a dangerous thing to pray; it might be that we even end up like Paul.

But we recognize this prayer of Paul's even more fully as something into which we still need to grow if we are to be like him, when he adds what the Cross of Christ meant to him personally. By it the world was crucified to him, and by it he was crucified to the world. The world, with everything that it stands for, had found the place where it belongs in the life of us all: nailed to Christ's Cross and therefore powerless to exert its pressures or its charms upon Paul. And Paul was equally crucified to the world by the fact of Christ's Cross, so that even when the old orders came and the old habits pulled hard, Paul couldn't do anything except hang where Christ had hung for him. The Cross held him so completely to the love of God that he was dead over against all that the world holds out as being life. God had forbidden that Paul glory in anything save the Cross of Christ. God was successful in answering Paul's prayer. Is this what we really want, we who live in such a delightful world of TV and wonderful vacations and glorious possibilities of self-expression? What would happen if God would take us literally and make us blind, physically blind, to everything except the Cross, so that wherever we would look there would be nothing for us and our sight except Christ's Cross, so that wherever we would reach out we would clasp nothing except the Cross, and wherever we would go we would be walking in the shadow of the Cross and would find our goal in the Cross? Should we change the prayer and ask for something less forbidding? Or should we change our hearts and our minds so that this would not be forbidding at all because of God? The latter is repentance, and it is actually this repentance that we pray for when we ask, not that God should change things for us, especially not the Cross and its centrality, but that God would change us so that the Cross of Christ can be central and thus be our only glory.

It is repentance that we are after under God in all these midweek services, the repentance that can be wrought only by the Cross of Christ, the repentance that lets all else go in order that we may truly glory in the Cross of Christ. God forbid everything that would prevent this! God grant us the faith to see:

The Cross of Christ My Power from God

"Father, not My will but Thine be done!" Thus Jesus had prayed, and His bloody sweat is the eternal evidence that He was in dead earnest that His Father's will be done at all or any cost to Himself. And it was the Father's will being done all the way through, unless we want to insist that God does not hear prayer because the Russians are right when they insist that with their probing into space they have blown up any throne that might have been in the sky; unless we want to say that God was not involved in the Passion and death of Jesus Christ so that God is in no way concerned about our salvation because He was in no way active in providing it. Our choices for or against the Christian faith are not merely in the great actions to which we give ourselves; they are first made in the little things, like our attitude toward prayer and therefore the frequency and the manner of our praying; like our manifest attitude toward God's Word, preached and written, as we openly show our involvement in what that Word speaks to us.

31

We believe with Jesus that all of it was the Father's will being done so that the shameful betrayal always has something to do with my own betrayal of Him and shows me how willingly and unwillingly I play the part of Judas over against my God. It was all the Father's will for His Son, which means God's will for our salvation, and if we would see the salvation from what, we look at the denials of Peter by which God shows us what is involved when we live and speak and do without even recognizing God and thereby insist that Jesus has no place and no part with us. We need to have Jesus look upon us out of this Passion of His which we ourselves caused, for only so will there yet be hope for us as we go out and weep bitterly. It was all the Father's will that was being done, and so we hear no protest from Jesus as God's court declares Him guilty, guilty of all things, of blasphemy. He was guilty with my guilt, and I am there given to see again what my sin is, my little sins and my big sins, my manner of dealing with those things which obviously cannot matter too much because I do them no differently than everybody else. That made Jesus guilty of blasphemy, which is the vilest evil against God.

This above all is what we need to see all the way through, that the Father's will was being done with regard to Christ and therefore by Christ. Only so do we know the love of God, not the cheap and painless love that we too often assume when we regard God as merely winking at our little frailties and all but smiling at the antics of His poor, dear, little children, but the terrible love that broke God's heart so that it might still enfold us and draw us and make of us what God would have us be; that terrible love that so loved us that it declared of its own Son that He was guilty of blasphemy, that Son in whom alone the Father could ever be well pleased.

32

Here is the true mystery of godliness, God made manifest in the flesh, this suffering, pain-ridden, shame-filled, despicable flesh that we know as Jesus in His Passion and death. Here is the one and only time where a "why" was in order, when Jesus had to cry out to His Father: "Why hast Thou forsaken Me!" Our *whys* are in the final analysis an impertinence because they reveal a claim on our part which we really have no right to make. Our *whys* really are our failure to recognize that God has given every answer that we can possibly need right here in Jesus Christ. If we still need something beyond that, then we deny the love of God, and God has no choice but to give us up to that other which we prefer beyond His love in Christ.

The Father's will is the Passion and death of Jesus Christ. Here is revelation at its fullest, and we pray God for seeing eyes and believing hearts that we might see and understand what is here given us. Something new enters the picture tonight as the will of God is unfolded for us in its relation to the world, the world of power as represented by Pontius Pilate. It may be that we would be able to unravel all the technicalities of this court scene and by all fair standards refuse to use the word *trial* because this was so manifestly a mistrial. But all that this would show would be that we were not taking seriously the prayer of Gethsemane, as if Jesus was not also doing the will of the Father before Pilate. If we want to insist on the mistrial end of it, we would have to say that this was not the first or the last time that this occurred, even under the vaunted Roman justice. But then we would only have to remember that that's what the world really is all about, constantly setting up its own judgments and standards and then claiming that they are the standards and judgments of God, having only

33

very partial insights but still claiming eternal validity for them, basically recognizing the wrong in any prejudice but so thoroughly prejudiced itself that it cannot possibly be just. But then be sure that you remember that we are part and parcel of this world and that this is equally true of us. And then be sure that you add that as little as you could expect anything better of a politician like Pilate, so little can you expect anything better from us who are ever on the same battle line of conflicting interests, which do more to influence our choices and our actions than any standard of justice in which we pride ourselves. Our right and wrong is always relative, and we know it if we recognize that our lives are not as right as we pretend, but are always more the effort to justify ourselves in giving reasons for doing what we know is wrong. We are all politicians like Pilate. This is what we see when Christ stands before Pilate and when Christ stands before us. His standing there reveals our need, our very deep need, for forgiveness.

But because the will of God was being carried out here and not only the will of Pilate, we are compelled to look further. Jesus Himself indicates that when He tells Pilate: "Thou wouldest have no power over Me except it were given thee from above." If God had withdrawn His power from Pilate, the man would have been helpless. If there was not some sense in which the power of Rome was the power of God, not even a fool would have referred to Rome as the Eternal City because it would have been buried under the ashes of forgottenness before it hardly came into being. This is what the world powers always forget, that they are what they are only by the grace of God and therefore for the use of God. But they always end up rising to the full heights of pride whereby they arrogantly assert that they won their own power and they carved out their own favorable place among the nations. This is always the beginning of the end because then God is no longer able to use the nation for those ends for which He raised it up, no longer able to use it except as a horrible example of what happens when nations exalt themselves against God and put themselves in the place of God.

And it always appears to be just the opposite of what it actually is so that God is known as the Ruler of the nations only by faith and God's ends are known to be served only by faith and God's ultimate victory is always being won only before the eyes of faith. Perhaps this more than anything else is to be seen as Jesus stands there before Pilate. There we have God's power, both in Jesus and in Pilate, for there is no power, none whatsoever, but of God. In Jesus we see the power of God used as God would have it used, in obedience to God and to the glory of God. In Pilate we see the power of God misused in that it is used for purely material ends and is not used to the glory of God. Let's be sure of this one thing: Pilate may have known that he was not doing the right thing in terms of stated justice, but he was also convinced that he was doing the best thing for the people over whom he had the supervision and therefore for the Roman Empire, which he served. In the long run, who would remember this one incident of this one man if only peace could be preserved, the famed Roman peace, if only the people could be kept satisfied so that they would not rebel? So Pilate, like all men, had his gods whom he served in spite of (or was it because of?) his somewhat sarcastic question: What is truth? Yes, what is truth when the pressure is on you so that if you do it one way you are damned and if you do it the other way you are equally damned! What is truth when the stakes

35

come so much higher than mere principle and the fate of nations hangs in the balance and the welfare of large numbers of people depends on your decision! Surely we know what that means, we who come under the same pressure on a smaller scale, we who know from personal experience that truth can soon be twisted out of its shape when personal interest is involved and can be bent at least a little bit when the desires of self pound through our minds and hearts so that we hear nothing else because it is part of the throbbing of our blood. We know what truth is, and so did Pilate. We merely ask, "What is truth?" as he did, when it suits our purposes not to be bound by it, not to be as truthful as we know how.

And here we see the difference between the power of God in Christ and the power of God in Pilate, who represents the world. God's power becomes the very power of the devil when it is seen and used apart from God's will, God's inflexible will, God's will which cannot be bent out of shape to fit the moment and our needs and the strong crying of our flesh. The moment, our needs, and our strong cryings must be bent and broken, if need be, to fit the will of God. That's why Jesus stands before Pilate at all, that God might put us all on trial in the trial — of whom? Amazingly, of Pilate! You never come into any kind of a contact with Jesus Christ but that you put Him on trial. But in the eyes of God, you are the one who is really on trial. Surely that is clear to us as Jesus stands before the Roman governor! Jesus begins to ask the questions, and like it or not, Pilate has to answer and thereby expose his own guilt. Jesus had been delivered by the Jews, Pilate claims, and thereby shows his own lack of implication, his own lack of involvement. But just that is his guilt: he tried not to be personally involved, so that he did not bother to look

36

into who this Jesus really was, to question and search and to seek if haply he might find God. If you claim to stand aloof, you are merely exposing your guilt because no one can stand aloof when God even claims to draw near. This is the sin of the world, and it is the sin of many church members. They think to keep themselves free of additional responsibility by not getting too involved. What they do not realize is that they are involved because God has involved them in Christ. What they are merely saying is that they will not have it God's way.

Here before Pilate we see the real nature of the Cross and its meaning to this day, because here is the power of God in Christ versus the power of the world in Pilate. How did it come out? The way it always does. God's power ends up on the Cross. Indeed, God's power is identified with the Cross. Why should this be? The devil suggested to Jesus that it could be different, with all doors flung open to Him and with all the might and the majesty of the world following in His train. All Jesus had to do was fall down and worship the devil and quit insisting on this rigid worship of God that refuses to see and do anything except God's will. But Jesus refused, and so He ends up before Pilate. Why always this way, this way even to this day? Because God's power is always saving power, the power of love, God's love, the power by which God draws men unto Himself and not the power by which God destroys men into our deserved hell. This is how the Cross of Christ is our power from God, for it is the power which God Himself gives us to believe in Him, to come to Him, to trust in Him to the denial of every other claim to our trust.

To them that perish the Cross of Christ is nothing but foolishness, just as surely as it was to Pilate. True, Jesus might give your wife bad dreams for a night or

37

two, and He might move you to a certain kind of admiration, but to exchange what you've got in order to have what He offers, to get out from under what is really ruling you now in order to be in His kingdom, who ever heard of something like that! Yes, who has? Surely we have not, unless the Cross of Christ has exerted its power upon us so that we own there our fault, our own fault, our own most grievous fault, and then listen to God's interpretation over the Cross: "I have loved you with an everlasting love, I have called you by your name, you are Mine!" This is the power of God, that you look at the Cross and behold the Lamb of God, which taketh away the sin of the world. The disciples didn't want it for Christ or for themselves, didn't want it any more than we do. They wanted the great Jewish dream of the restoration of the kingdom of David, the kingdom of pomp and splendor and lording it over others, so that they insisted that any reference to the Cross should be far from Christ. They did not want it until it became God's power to them, and then they became men who had only one theme: "In the Cross of Christ I Glory!" When the Cross of Jesus Christ is the power of God to us, we look, we worship, we adore, because to us then it will mean but one thing: "He loved me and gave Himself for me!" Such power will it be to us that it will so turn our lives and thoughts and values upside down that we pray and mean for God to bring just this about when we say: "God forbid that I should glory save in the Cross of our Lord Jesus Christ, by whom the world is crucified unto me, and I unto the world." Heavenly Father, give us the grace so to pray, and hear our prayer by making the Cross of Christ Thy power unto us, even Thy power unto salvation, so that we believe in Him who hangs there for us. Amen.

38

THE CROSS OF CHRIST
My Wisdom of God

Matt. 27:17
in the light of
1 Cor. 1:21

When St. Paul attempted to convey the heart of his preaching among the Corinthians, he let us look deep into the source of his power and even more deeply into the source from which he drew all of his mighty themes. Here it is for whatever we would do with it and for whatever end we would use it, if haply we are at all interested in achieving the same ends as the great persecutor become even greater apostle: "I determined to know nothing among you save Jesus Christ and Him crucified!" As in so many other instances in the Scriptures and as with so many other expressions that go to the very heart of the Christian faith, this one also seems to be somewhat overstated, so that without at least some modification it cannot stand there in all of its bare claim and it cannot possibly convey what the naked meaning of the words would seem to intend. After all, you need only read the balance of the letter to see that Paul knew a great deal more among these very Corinthians than Jesus Christ and Him crucified! That sounds good when you read it and when you would introduce your own ministry to people who still don't know you and when you would attempt to get someone interested in the Christian faith. Then it all sounds so simple and so loving and so inviting, but once in, you find out that it never is that way, and once a pastor has been at a place for some time it is only too apparent that other things are emphasized besides the Crucified.

39

And the first thing you know, you are involved in all sorts of demands for your money, your time, and for something that you tried to get away from when you began to investigate the Christian faith and first thought that this church might have something more to offer than what you were accustomed to elsewhere.

Whatever we may say about ourselves and our own reaction to something as blunt as this, we should be very careful that we do not attempt to hang the apostle on the basis of accusations which properly are directed toward ourselves. It may well be that we do not take the claims of Scripture as seriously as they intend themselves to be taken, but this only tells us something about ourselves and not the claims of the Scriptures. We may have grown so accustomed to taking everything that we ever hear, because of the wild claims of people and advertising, in something less than the sense which the words convey, with something more than one grain of salt, that we might habitually do the same when we read the Scriptures. But this merely shows what kind of people we have become without even intending to, and it does not show what the Scriptures have become in the light of modern and better knowledge. We are the ones who are at fault, and if we will but examine carefully, we will see that we are always tempted to interpret the Scriptures in such a way that we take the sting out of what they say and we can hear it all with the same bland unconcern with which we listen to the many other things that really don't concern us after all. We would never determine to know nothing save Jesus Christ and Him crucified because we are so sure that there is so very much else as well; we simply could not stand it because we are unwilling to be crucified ourselves, unwilling to be a sacrifice in whole or in part to the welfare of
40

our neighbor and the glory of God. It isn't really the theme at all that prevents us; it is ourselves whose hearts are still so scattered over the landscape of this world that they could not possibly be single, so single in Christ that all else would be excluded.

This precisely is what had taken place for Paul, and this is the only reason why he not only could say what he did but actually meant it so fully that he really was that way and really acted that way and really spoke that way. But you don't simply fall into that sort of thing like rolling off a log. It took real determination on Paul's part because there was so much else that cried and clamored so loud for expression. When you read this brief theme in its entire setting, you can almost see the tears which it caused Paul to weep, the agonizing prayers in which he engaged because the whole pull of his life was in the opposite direction, the constant no with which he had to keep beating his own natural bents and desires to bring them into submission to the Cross of Christ. This we are not willing to do. In fact, ask yourself if you have the courage and the faith to pray God that He would bring you to this, that He would dedicate you so unreservedly, so unqualifiedly, so wholly, to the Crucified that henceforth you determine to know nothing else. And yet it is for just this that we are praying again tonight. It is just this that we would have God press home upon us in such a way that we have no avenue left down which we can run from Him and no valid excuse that we would be willing to hold up when He confronts us with His total claim upon our total selves in the Crucified. God, detour us from the bypaths down which our own weak wills would lead us.

God, help us to Thine own ends as we tonight consider:

The Cross of Christ My Wisdom of God

Paul was certainly no fool. Regardless of whether you accept the truth of the epistle, you at least must recognize that the writer of Romans had more than the ordinary amount of brains. In fact, quite apart from their theme, all the epistles of Paul must rank among the great writings of the world. And after all these years you don't maintain such a high place among the achievements of men by being an idiot. But we are wrong if we press that too hard, because then we are pressuring in the very direction that Paul himself wanted to avoid. He knew that about himself. No one had to tell him that he could well hold his own with the wise of his day or of any other day, so that he could have confidently entered the arena of our times and have been the victor more often than defeated on the basis of simple IQ. But this very thing was his ongoing battle with himself calling for all the determination which his new life and new outlook in Christ could possibly muster. When he was attacked, do you suppose it was easy for him not to respond in kind, not to lash out with the same bitter sarcasm with which he was cut, not to overwhelm with a better learning than that which was so obviously being displayed? The most difficult thing in the world is to be truly superior and not parade your superiority, especially before those who regard you as pretty stupid, before those who obviously are so taken with their own brain power that a display of counterforce would seem to be just what they need. But Paul steadfastly refused to do it. Why?

Here is where we must be doubly careful, so that we don't come up with something that we regard as a kind of tactic, a method, an approach, on the part of Paul, that in itself promises greater success than any other way. Paul

42

couldn't do anything else because he was caught, completely caught, ever since Christ permitted him to get up out of the dust whither he had been so terribly humbled before the troop that he was leading. Nothing really made any difference to Paul any more, nothing at all, except Jesus Christ and Him crucified. What good for a man to be proved wrong in his arguments if his wrongness is not seen in the light of the Cross? What good to overwhelm a man with your logic if he does not submit to the power of the Cross? What good for a man to end up admitting that you are more brilliant than he is if the brilliance of God in the face of the Crucified Jesus sheds no glory into his heart and no hope into his life? And so we could keep on and on with questions until we had exhausted our last possible expression of personal superiority over another. Yet it would benefit no one, not even you, except for your pride, if God's superiority in Jesus Christ had not been established. And this is something which only God can do, even as He Himself had to do it for us; otherwise we still have not been brought to bow beneath the Cross. And just this is the way that God does it, the way He always did it, the one way in which the religious and the wise will not have Him because they still want to be what they themselves are by themselves, religious and wise.

There are those who have openly spoken about the cruelty of God, and they have enough evidence to point to in order to make a case. There are those of us who wouldn't say that sort of thing openly but who often harbor genuine doubts in this area, especially when our own backs are up against the wall and we know them to be pressed there by God Himself, and we receive no other word than this: "Read Job and Jeremiah, and simply endure!" But regardless of what we may want to point to as evidence for our accusation, the one place where it would appear

43

most justified is the way God must first empty us of everything before He gives us a thing; the way God must first utterly crush us before He will raise us up; the way God must first reveal everything else in its folly before the Cross of Christ becomes His wisdom to us. Why can't we have both? Why must the break always be so complete? Why must the fact of God always be so brutal? Why must the confrontation always be a demand for an either/or and never the possibility of both/and? Why must this be the only choice: "He that is not with Me is against Me, and he that gathereth not with Me scattereth abroad"?

The problem, as always, is not with God or His Christ, but with ourselves. There seems to be something harsh about this, not because God is harsh but because we refuse to be corrected, even by God's love. There is something here that hurts us, not because God hurts us but because He must pull us away from that which will surely destroy us, and we won't let go, and neither will He. There is something very offensive to us here, not because God is impolite but because He is God and we are always operating with our own little gods who are false and therefore must be destroyed if God is to be God to us. Cruel, we say? Is it cruel to plunge a knife into your stomach? Of course it is. But what when a surgeon does it to cut out the cancer? Is it cruel to keep your wounds open, to press upon them so that you can hardly stand the pain? Of course it is, and it reminds us of some of the stories that came out of the concentration camps. But what if the wound is kept open to permit it to drain, and it is gauze that is pressed in over and over again to absorb the poison so that the healing is not merely a smooth exterior but also healing from within? No, the gods that are really cruel are the gods which are made by men, the gods which

44

permit us to do precisely as we please with no concern for our future; the gods that even give us the power to destroy ourselves and never interfere as long as we are having fun; the gods who add fuel to fires of our self-styled wisdom until we consume ourselves and the world from which we draw our wisdom. If God were what many pretend, He would never hurt us. He just wouldn't care! He would never expose our folly by the Cross of Christ. There would never be a Cross of Christ because God would refuse to become that personally involved with people like us!

The Cross of Christ is the wisdom of God, God's infinitely wise way of healing us of our diseases and making it possible for us to be forgiven and come back to God. It is also the full wisdom that is given to us with regard to God, even making us wise unto salvation through faith which is in Christ Jesus. Apart from the Cross of Christ we are still fools over against God because then we still say in our hearts that that could never be the way of God. Apart from the Cross of Christ we are still trapped in that wisdom of the world which is the denial of God, because that is characteristic of it. It always denies God as God is because it would always make Him over into what it wants, and that's what makes it the world in its enmity against God. St. Paul reminds us that God can be known from the creation of the world, even His eternal power and Godhead, because He did not leave Himself without a witness. But what happened? The wrath of God has to be revealed from heaven because man holds the truth of God down in unrighteousness, simply refuses to recognize God because he wants to live it his own way against God and then looks around for all sorts of reasons why he can deny God or despise God or make a fool of God. And such also are we, and from that God would win us again, and for that God Himself raised the Cross of Christ to reveal His wisdom and thereby cancel out our folly. And every time God brings us to the Cross again, the folly is exposed for what it is, the gauze is pressed deeper and harder into the wounds, the knife is plunged again to lay bare the foul malignancy that would consume us even under the very Cross of Christ.

This is why we are brought to stand there, and this is why Lent is a penitential season, the season of admitted hurt and being wounded and confessed folly, because then especially are we made to see the wisdom of God in the Cross, we are made to see ourselves personally involved. Pilate, the manipulating politician, the advocate of expediency, already reveals our folly in connection with Christ, and in him we are condemned not for lacking God's principles but especially for knowing and not doing, taught of God but not walking in the light of what God teaches. This is the sort of thing that always condemns Christ to death in a man's life, even while he insists that he has the highest regard for Jesus, even though he strikes upon some expedient like washing his hands to convince himself that he is innocent of Christ's blood. Look well — to what? We like to think that with regard to God we need only look well to what we say when we are consciously before Him, so that it all comes out in such a way that in general at least it matches the Bible. Pilate must remind each of us that we look well to our dealings with other people if we want to determine what we are going to do with Jesus, which is called Christ; that we look well to what we do in our jobs — after all, Pilate was engaged in his job when Christ was brought before him — if we want to determine whether we are going to crucify Jesus or not; that we look well always to where we are because, whether we recognize it or not, we are always on trial before Christ.

46

But even in his grasping at straws, even in his clever devising of expedients by which he hoped to get himself off the hook, Pilate is still the servant of God because the powers that be are ordained of God. Pilate may think that he is especially clever when he comes up with the idea of giving the people a choice between Jesus and the worst criminal in his dungeons, but it is still God who is doing the revealing of His wisdom. Our folly must be exposed to its depths, even the folly of people who have the reputation of being good and kind and otherwise religious. This is what we dare not forget ever in our viewing of the Passion of Jesus: God was involved because it was His doing and the revealing of His wisdom. But in order to have it be what He wanted, it had to be done by the best of people and not by the scum of the earth, from whom nobody would expect anything different. In other words, it had to be done in such a way that not one of us could find an out for himself and excuse himself politely by saying that it is all too vulgar for his participation and too bloody for him to look too closely. Everyone is there, even the best of us, and especially the best of us, and the only ones who beg off are those who are not willing to have themselves condemned. They still want to be wise with their own wisdom and refuse to let the wisdom of God condemn their folly; then they merely condemn themselves to be fools forever.

What gets into people that something like this before Pilate could be possible? There stands Jesus, known to the people not only for His claims but also for His deeds of mercy among them and His earnest pleas for them to return to God and be healed and saved. Alongside Him stands Barabbas, only briefly characterized by the Scriptures but with that little shown to have been involved in sedition at least and possibly even murder. Part of that was what Jesus had been accused of when they said He made Himself a king, and this was what was supposed to have incensed the leaders of the Jews so much that they demanded Jesus should be crucified. Here Barabbas was known by everyone actually to be guilty of sedition. And what happens when the people, these religious people, these very best people that God Himself had been able to produce through a long history of revelation and promise, are given a choice? They choose Barabbas and demand Jesus' crucifixion. How do you account for something like that? How could they do something like that when not too long before they must have been on their knees in prayer and were looking forward so much to celebrating the great feast of the Passover that they would not even go into Pilate's court, lest they break one of their laws and therefore be prevented from eating the Passover? We hear the sound of many contradictions by simply stating the questions, and we come up with no answer — unless we already know ourselves and our terrible contraditions and our own religious scruples which we hold to so very firmly even when we deny the very heart of our religion. Even now sin lieth like a great beast slumbering in our hearts, a terrible beast that can be aroused in a moment by anger or by lust to rend and tear everything that gets in its way, even our own selves. As long as we live, that great beast is within us, and we will never handle it by ourselves. It can be kept under control only by the power and wisdom of the Cross of Christ. Another way of putting it is that all of our wisdom is folly after all, at best able to deal with mistakes, but altogether incapable of dealing with such things as demons and sin and guilt. Our own wisdom is no match for our passions and cannot even keep a good check on our desires and give us more than innocuous answers when we are aroused and inflamed by prejudices

48

and the fanning of our ego. That's when and that's why we choose Barabbas and insist that Jesus should be crucified. That's the opening of the old wound every time we look in here, and that's the hurt to our pride of wisdom whenever we are brought up against what God insists in His wisdom, the Cross of Christ. That's the story of my life, choosing Barabbas even when I know better, still actually lusting after what Barabbas represents even when with my mouth I sing and claim Jesus Christ. And if we still refuse to admit that of ourselves, we are still fools and refuse to admit the Cross of Christ as the wisdom of God.

But if we admit it, if we truly see ourselves howling with that maddened mob of truly good people, then let the "Crucify Him! Crucify Him!" really mean something. Let it be the expression of God's wisdom through us, the recognition that nothing less than that offering of the Son of God could adequately deal with what I am. I've chosen Barabbas because that's what I myself am in my heart of hearts and not the gay, clever, wise leader of a congregation. I cried "Crucify!" when God confronted me in the wisdom of His Son. I insisted so much that I helped send Him to the Cross. But this is the wisdom of God: He trapped me in my own wisdom and made it foolishness. He acceded to my demands and — and what? He overwhelmed me by the wisdom of His love. Christ went whither I sent Him in my folly, and now He invites me: Come unto Me, and I will give thee rest; come whither thou thyself didst send Me, and I will make thee wise with the wisdom of God. Tell me, those of you who have stood there, what else can I do now but come to Him! Tell me, what else can I do now except determine to know nothing save Jesus Christ and Him crucified! Amen.

THE CROSS OF CHRIST
My Peace with God

> *Luke 23:27-31*
> *in the light of*
> *Phil. 4:7*

Boldly we said it! Bravely we meant it! Unlike Peter we not only were forewarned by the words of our Lord, but we were given to see the dangers to which we would be exposed, the all but uncontrollable surge for expression on the part of our desires, the all but irresistible pull by which all of our contacts would drag us away. Unlike James and John we harbored no false dreams of mighty conquest and sitting one on the right and the other on the left of the throne of power, so that it never even occurs to us as it did to them to call down fire from heaven in order to destroy the opposition which we encounter. We saw that the gate was narrow, and before we went in we dropped many a thing that would not permit us to stoop low enough so that we could enter. We had looked down the broad way, the pleasant way, and we saw it literally teeming with throngs as on a picnic, and we knew what it meant by comparison to set foot on the narrow way where you walk so largely alone and where almost every step makes you cry out in anguish as your feet grow all bloody and raw and you can summon no reason from within why you should continue. We beheld the whole gruesome drama unfold before our eyes, the drama that is so easily referred to as the Passion and death of our Lord Jesus Christ but is so very hard to enter into because we would make it a matter of our imaginations and not of our hearts. But we beheld it

50

from the first bloody drop of sweat in Gethsemane to the final piercing of the side out of which fairly gushed forth blood and water, and we were bluntly told that not only was this God's inestimable gift to us but Christ also suffered for us, leaving us an example that we should follow in His steps. But in the face of it all we still insisted that that was for us. If that's what it meant to be a Christian, then even so I would be a Christian. If that's what was involved in discipleship, count me in, Lord, because I herewith declare myself Thy disciple.

But where has it all come out? We would have to be the first to admit that with far greater knowledge than Peter, we still never come out any better than Peter; with far greater insights into the purpose of Christ's coming than James and John we still have blundered just as badly. We stand before Christ and Barabbas, and we are made to see very clearly what is involved in our choices, and we have to confess that our wisdom is always such folly that we choose Barabbas. This is our sin against God, that we continue to insist on having it our way and not His way. So we confess the sin again as we did last Wednesday, and we are brought once more to bow beneath the Cross of Christ as the wisdom of God. With that we did not merely say, however, what is wrong with us, nor did we merely confess that we stoop here alone as the one place of having it all set right again, but we get up from our knees with our eyes more widely opened to what is involved in our daily involvements and with our hearts more firmly set on practicing the presence of our Lord and our minds more fixed than ever in their determination to know nothing save Jesus Christ and Him crucified so that we live by the wisdom of God. Did we mean what we said? If tears could spell out sincerity, we would cry a river of them to manifest

51

that this was our most genuine intent. If at the moment Christ would have asked it, we would have died with Him but would not have denied Him in any wise or chosen the safety of our own hides over the confession of His name, much less have chosen Barabbas as the fullest expression of what our life is all about while we send Jesus off to be crucified. We meant it just as fully as we meant anything!

But now, for all of our meaning of it, how many of us even got home last Wednesday evening without forgetting what we had meant so fully, without actually denying our Lord, without actually choosing for Barabbas? Would any of us care to give a moment-by-moment account of our lives since last Wednesday, all the while consciously standing in Pilate's court with this deed and that action and those words held up as determining for or against Christ? If repentance is exemplified by Peter as he goes out and weeps bitterly, we could hardly take a step any more without having to weep, we could hardly see any more for being blinded by our regret at having looked the way we did. Is there never anything different for us as long as we live? Is it always to be a coming back to the very One whom we said we would never leave? Is it always going over the same ground that we have covered so often that we have literally worn a path of shortcut to our many trespasses?

This is the great problem of the Christian life, note well, the *Christian* life, because it is not a problem for life in general. Life in general can never be untrue to its resolves for God; what makes it life in general is that it resolves only for itself and not for God. The Christian life is always a resolving for God, and it must always be a resolving anew. It is always on the way only, and
52

this side of death never actually arrives. It chooses, and by its faith it chooses Christ, but then it must choose all over again for Him because in fact and in expression it has chosen Barabbas. If we fail to see this, we will end up in despair or hypocrisy: despair because we never seem to attain, and we know that we must attain if we are to live; hypocrisy if we convince ourselves that we have attained because our lives are not as obviously Barabbas-styled as the headline lives in our newspapers. The Christian life is altogether the life of repentance, constant repentance, genuine repentance, because it is ongoing; sincere repentance because there is never a moment it is Christian unless it pleads: "God, be merciful to me, a sinner!" This is the last warning that the Christian faith has for us all: "Let him that thinketh he standeth take heed lest he fall." Your resolves are never enough, your desperate efforts to change will never bring it off, your firing yourself up will never create the heat and the energy needed. This is why we disown our own wisdom and look to the Cross in order to be made wise with the wisdom of God. And that's what the whole Christian life is, of God and through God and to God, so that there is nothing whatever that you can say about it as Christian but what you are declaring what it is by Christ, what is different about it because of what it is of God. Luther once said that you don't have to command a rock lying in the sun to be warm. We must always be in the sunshine of God's grace in Christ Jesus if we are to be warmed and give off the heat that expresses Christ. This has been our attempt this Lenten season as all of our interpretations of the Cross have come from God and ended up with God. We pray that God would warm us again this evening by His grace as we consider:

53

The Cross of Christ My Peace with God

"I will put enmity between thee and the woman," thus God had promised when He cursed the devil forever for destroying God's most magnificent work — man. We cannot even imagine what life was like without sin, perfect harmony between God and man, perfect response of love to the love with which God loved man, perfect peace because there wasn't a thing wrong between God and man and God walked with man as a man walks with his friend. Now suddenly all that was disrupted, and God's intentions were distorted, and man declared himself a rebel, galled by what now came to him as the unwarranted authority of God, jealous within his heart of hearts of the Godness of God to which he himself could not attain. A rebel, a revolutionary, against God because he had chosen sides with the devil, because he had listened to the devil's way of becoming like God and thereby was won over to the unholy alliance of all that stands in perpetual opposition to God. And with that man destroyed his peace with God and, certainly without intending it, he thereby destroyed the peace of God's creation and gave himself over to the curse of Cain because he became a fugitive and a vagabond on the earth. Ever since man listened to the devil he has been running away, no less from himself than from God, running away from the destiny he was created for in order that he might embrace the destruction which he made for himself. Ever since man was convinced that you can become like God Himself if you only assert yourself and be independent of God, he has had no home, for our souls must ever be restless till they find their rest in God. Yet man, restless searcher, supposed rest was his to find and not a waiting gift of God.

What should God do? We always are so certain that we can improve on God's way, and intrinsic to our sin is wanting to make the choices which only God can and must make. Examine yourself, and see how you would react to something like that if you were God and had the power and the authority of God and it were so flagrantly opposed, so despised in every evidence of love which you showed, man so fully and finally insistent on going his own way and doing what he wanted to do. Here is really a fine opportunity to assess what life would really be like if man could have his way and man could really do what only God can do. What would you have done if you actually were God? Let's not be too hasty in answering with words lest our present deeds have to shout them down as a lie. The real fact of the matter is that we do at least act as gods in our human relationships and by the manner we treat each other we constantly show the kind of gods we would like to be. Would you set out, as God did, on the long road of winning man back by putting enmity between him and the devil, or would you denounce the enmity and let man eat its bitter fruit? The answer to that might well be found not in what you would say now but in what you said or did not say to the person who hurt your feelings, in what you did or refused to do in order to work out a genuine reconciliation under total forgiveness. The answer to that might better be found in how well you pray the Fifth Petition, in how interested you are in putting enmity between the devil and your fellowman by saving him from his destruction, in how you live it as though you were all alone on some self-erected throne or in genuine concern and redeeming love for those who need your praying hand and your supporting hand and your giving hand. God who is the true and the living

55

God does not respond in kind, does not give as good as He gets, does not hold Himself aloof from men in majestic unconcern and self-concern. He is the God who broke the enmity between Himself and man, the enmity which man himself had created. God broke it by putting enmity between man and his real enemies, so that man might not be at peace with his destroyers but that man might be at peace again with the God whom he would have destroyed. This is the peace of God because it is peace which only God, the offended One, can create. And this is the peace of God which is His gift to us in the Cross of His Son Jesus Christ.

Pilate refused to make a choice, and with that he made his choice. You just can't let someone else crucify Jesus without being involved yourself, even though you do have some ready expedient with which you can clear your conscience. The people may stand by and heap curses and imprecations upon themselves to the effect that Jesus' blood be upon them and their children; it also is upon us if we do not stand up in the name of Christ and refuse to permit it unless they are willing to do the same to us. This is only the interpretation of Christ's own word: "Whosoever shall deny Me before men, him will I also deny before My Father which is in heaven." What else is that except His blood being visited upon us? But Pilate would be neither warned nor won, so that while he was perfectly willing to speculate about Christ and God and truth, he was unwilling to commit himself to such a degree as to give up everything that was holding him back: his position, his being a friend of Caesar, his ambition to get ahead. This is when the Cross always finally appears as the place whither such men would send the Christ while they get on with their self-seeking, which is enmity against God.

56

The Cross itself had been ready for some time, always ready even from eternity, because it is not only Pilate's and my enmity against Christ being my Lord and my God, but it is also God's love. If we could only see this once in faith, that God is not God by overpowering us or our enmity, by overwhelming our duller senses and treating our nerves to a good dose of shock therapy, by being God to us as we would be gods to our fellowmen. He is God in love, love beyond our understanding, love beyond our telling, love that must be seen and known in Jesus Christ before it can be believed. Man fashions that Cross for God, and God takes the Cross and out of it fashions salvation for men. Men sin and express their defiance of God, and God takes their sin and their defiance and makes His grace abound all the more where these abound. Men mock God in Christ with the crown of thorns and the dirty purple and the reed scepter, and God takes the mockery and with it becomes the true Lord of sinners. Men insult God in His Son by numbering Him among the transgressors and putting Him in the middle as the archtransgressor against all that is holy among men and before God, and God takes it to convince us that His Son is truly numbered among us and is like us and therefore is for us. Man renews the warfare with God daily as he daily gives himself over to his opposition against God in Christ, and God makes peace possible by destroying the enmity of man's enmity and having nothing but double for all man's opposition, not double opposition but double yearning and pleading and winning to restore peace with man. All that is the Cross of Christ for us if we will own our participation there and if we will let that Cross be planted on that Calvary which is the place of the skull, the place of death, the place that is our own heart. Come, then, ye Simons out of Cyrene, who only came to worship God, to celebrate His great feast of the Passover; come, and let the Cross of Christ be laid upon your shoulders where it belongs, for only so will God be able to answer the real plea of our worship and give us deliverance beyond anything that once took place in Egypt! Come and let the powers of God's Holy Law thrust the Cross upon your conscience so that you can never get out from under it, and you will know that it was your burden in His Passion that Christ has borne for you. That's why your bearing the Cross now is your following of Jesus, the only peace with God that there is.

That, of course, is not the only possibility open to us. It never is. You see what can happen if you have a religion of your own making, a religion that is not relationship with God through Jesus Christ alone. Not only do you have to get this Jesus out of your religious way, then, but the Cross becomes the final hurdle that you will never master, because it is an offense to your morality, a stumbling block on which you break your religious neck because you refuse to carry it as your very real and personal guilt before God. Then you stand alongside the roadway of life which is always the Way of Sorrows for the Son of God if He is to walk it with us and for us, and you refuse to become involved with Him; you refuse to identify yourself with Him. You mock His stumbling, collapsing efforts to carry away what God says is rightfully yours. You won't turn a finger for Him, not even now, but are done with Him when the miracles cease for your benefit and the Cross comes into view, done with Him when there is no apparent benefit in it for you but only cost and personal self-denial and total self-sacrifice. Remember always that we are not now talking about the Romans, people outside the church; we are talking about those within the church, those who claimed to be under the

58

covenant of God, like you and me the baptized and the keepers of holy days and the strong regarders of the Bible as a book which we can handle but never as a book which must handle us. Oh, that we would get under that Cross with Christ and let our shoulders take the place of Simon's! You ask how is this possible? Only be faithful to the Christ of the Cross in all of life, only let Him have His will and His way to the crushing of your own and the destruction of the world's and the halting of the devil's, and you will quit asking how this can be possible today. You will know because you will no longer stand on the sidelines as a spectator; Christ's life and death will re-express their reality through you, also the shameful, painful walk to Calvary on our day's Via Dolorosa.

But there is another way, a way so bad that it calls forth the strongest possible warning and judgment from the very Jesus who is on His way to die for the people to whom He so spoke. You see, everything and anything is not just all right because we have the kind and gentle Jesus, who takes all our sin away. There are some things which make this impossible because they will not let Him be the Savior to us. For all their pious expression they keep Christ from being our Lord, which means also Lord of our sin. What happened on the Via Dolorosa to call forth the strong judgment of our text? Some women followed after Jesus and bewailed Him. They went into mourning for Him. He presented such a ghastly, helpless sight that their tender woman hearts could not but spill over in tears. And all they got for their pains is: "Weep not for Me, but weep for yourselves and for your children . . . for if they do these things in the Green Tree, what shall be done in the dry?" Beware, ye observers of Lent, ye walkers on the Way of Sorrows with Jesus, ye watchers at Calvary! Weeping for this poor Jesus will cause Him to speak judgment upon you. Lenten observances that do not pass over into daily life will one day give you reason to cry out for the mountains to fall upon you. Special responses and reactions to the Jesus of the Passion that do not recognize and own Him Savior, Savior at such a terrible price because of the terribleness of my transgression, the unutterable horror from which each one of us has to be saved, will bring this same thing upon you that was visited upon this Green Tree, this Holy One of God, and will utterly consume you if you are dried branches fit only for the fire, dried up over against God and man because you were not grafted into the only Vine, this Jesus Christ.

Weep we will because weep we must, but the weeping will be for ourselves and for our children. We brought that woe on Him, we, the wonderful people we always show ourselves to be, we the wonderful friends of God! But now the tears have been caused by God Himself, and they become tears of repentance, tears of unspeakable regret that I should have done that to my Lord and my God, tears because, however unimaginable, I did it, and off He goes bearing His Cross, my Cross, my personal hatred of God and my personal enmity against God. That's what I now see my sin to be. And with that the way of Christ's sorrows becomes the way of my return to God, and the curses with which I cursed Him and the mockery with which I sinned against Him fall back upon me from the forgiving God as blessing in Christ Jesus, as my eternal peace with my heavenly Father. Look with that faith, and see through such enlightened eyes, and you will hear the eternal benediction upon you, the sinner: The Lord bless thee, and keep thee, bless thee by the Cross, and keep thee always under the Cross; the

60

Lord make His face shine upon thee, the face all spattered with blood and spittle and covered with shame, that you might have in Christ the God who is gracious unto thee; the Lord lift up His countenance upon thee, His whole Being, there in Christ, and there wholly and fully for thee; and give thee peace, God's own peace, which man can never understand but which alone can keep our hearts and our minds through Christ Jesus. Amen.

THE CROSS OF CHRIST
My Salvation from God

Matt. 27:34-38
in the light of
1 Cor. 1:30, 31

"If they do these things in the Green Tree, what shall
be done in the dry?" This is the reason for taking a look
at yourself and your children, comparing what you see
there with what you are able to see in Jesus as He staggers
along the Way of Sorrows, and not weeping in pity over
Him but bitterly bewailing and lamenting what is laid bare
to such an honest look at yourselves and your children.
True, Jesus never wanted any man's pity. Pity is the gross-
est misunderstanding of all and simply refuses to look at
Jesus in the light of what He claims for Himself. True,
Jesus was attempting to shock these people into an insight
into themselves by which they would be brought down
from their heights of theoretical participation, down into
the arena of personal and direct involvement. But remember, Jesus never did or said anything merely for effect.
Unlike us, He not only always spoke the absolute truth
but was Himself the Truth, so that looking at Him and seeing yourself in comparison with Him is always judgment
upon self, judgment which we are unwilling to accept because we would rather cry over Him than see Him walking what is really our way; we would rather pity Him than
listen to Him. Here we are given some sort of notion of
what our way through life is like when we try to walk it
all by ourselves. It is the Way of Sorrows; it is the way
from judgment to exquisite torture; it is the way that we
really cannot walk alone with our burden, but on which

62

we stumble and fall and need help, though in our pride we insist on our self-sufficiency. All this that you see there — the anguish, the pain, the blood, the weakness unto fainting — all that is being done to the Green Tree, and He could just barely make it; He is in such straits that to see Him is to weep over Him. What, then, shall be done in the dry? What shall we see when our eyes are opened to behold ourselves walking this way that has only one out? How shall we endure when it cost Him His very life!

Of course, this doesn't make much sense unless we believe that Jesus actually was the Green Tree. Otherwise we have only a tragedy here, a kind of drama that shows us how bad it can get with men and how life is not always as fair and as kind as we might hope it to be; but then, that is fate, and you've got to take the bitter with the sweet, the wars with the peace, the death with the birth of loved ones. That doesn't sound too bad if you are on the outside looking in; if you are merely paying a visit to someone who is having a rough time of it, but are not yourself involved in a rough time that you can hardly handle any more. That even sounds brave, master-of-my-fate and captain-of-my-soul brave, until you yourself are under the cross which you cannot bear any longer, and you yourself are the one who has to do the weeping for yourself or your children, and you yourself sit in the mourner's bench shocked and dazed as you look into the coffin of your loved one, and you yourself lie there in the bed from which you cannot answer any more but can only stare and know what is meant when the doctor sadly shakes his head to others who are standing there weeping over you. Then all the brave TV shows that you ever saw and all the brave words that you heard and all the brave "keep a stiff upper lip" advice that you ever gave will sound pretty empty, more like a very hollow echo from afar of words that you should

63

have listened to long ago: "Thou fool, this night thy soul shall be required of thee; then whose shall all those things be that thou didst trust in?"

But there is only one reason why we are here at all: we believe that this is being done to the Green Tree, the one Tree that has life in Himself, the one Tree that can still bring forth fruit for God, that is acceptable to God. And mind you, this is His own claim about Himself when He was in His very worst condition. He still believes, in spite of all appearances to the contrary, that the Word of God is still true: "This is My beloved Son, in whom I am well pleased!" About not one of us could God say that, only about this One, to whom all this was being done. What, then, would all this do to us, the dry branches? What when the terrible fires of judgment, which are here licking at the Son of God Himself, finally reach out for us? Fire can scorch and scar a green tree, but it will utterly consume dry trees. We do well to weep under the Cross, but for ourselves and for our children: not pity for Him, but repentance for ourselves; not some sentimental "Isn't that too bad?" but "My God, what have I done?" This is the only way that this mighty Sufferer can turn and not speak judgment upon us. Only so can He actually invite us in under His Cross in order that He might bless us forever. We pray that He would do just that this evening as we consider:

The Cross of Christ My Salvation from God

And they crucified Him. That's about all the evangelists tell us. Nothing about what was going on in the mind of Jesus. Nothing about the spikes, the hammer, the soldier who handled them. Nothing about the expression on Jesus' face when the nails pierced His tender skin

64

and the rejection of men and God pierced His most sensitive soul. Nothing about the brutal thump with which the Cross was thrust into its hole in order that this blasphemer might hang between God and men, heaven and earth, disowned by both and obviously well cursed for what must surely have been the ultimate in guilt. Nothing, except the fact of the crucifixion, because it is all for us. Let the shallow-minded find here nothing but what is found in every martyr's death: We know from the silence about it all, even from its sameness to the crucifixion of the two transgressors with Him, that this is the crucifixion of the Son of God. Surely all the elements were there for building up to a tragedy that our minds and hearts could hardly endure, so that if the men who wrote were merely interested in getting us to accept some invention, something by which they were intending to profit from us, then how could they forebear pulling all the stops with which humans are ordinarily moved? How could they refrain from psychologizing and attempting to give a grimace-by-grimace account of what was going through Jesus' mind and heart? How could they keep themselves from interspersing the account with all sorts of gasps and sighs that would enliven our imagination to a fuller grasp of the picture? But all we have is: "And they crucified Him." There is this same reticence about all His life; His birth in the stable with none of the heartrending accompaniments; the flight into Egypt with not a word about the hardships; His tremendous disappointment evidenced in His question with which He asks His disciples of all time, "Will ye also go away?" But none of the heroics, none of the dramatics, nothing that strives for effect. We have to do with God here, and it is to Him that we are drawn by the whole account, or it is from Him that we are repelled. But there is nothing, absolutely nothing, simply to move us, to thrill

65

us for a moment, to cause our nerve ends to tingle and the back of our necks to prickle. It is kept simple because it is simple confrontation by God, so that we here respond to God, or our response is unbelief in God. It is God still setting the terms and in no way consulting us about the terms; it is God giving us the straight facts of Himself in Christ without first inquiring what gilding might make the facts more acceptable to us.

But isn't there something else there as well? If that is God in Christ, the God-man Jesus, then it is God who has run headlong into man. And who was broken? This is the most amazing thing that there is about the Christian God. You can say everything and anything that you wish, reaching out as far into expressions as man can possibly reach, stretching and straining and all but breaking our poor human language in an effort to say something that is utterly beyond man's saying, you still haven't said what is decisive about the Christian God. Here in the crucifixion it is made altogether clear to us. Here is our God, able and willing to suffer; not God remote and unmoved and unmovable; not the God of perpetual rest, but the God who seeks man until He finds man, the God who takes into His own heart the hurt of man, the God who literally is smashed to pieces on man. This is what makes the Cross the climax that it is and that we all as Christians somehow sense. It is the high point of the Bible because everything else has been heading toward it. Here is God, who made the initial decision with regard to fallen man, then and there declaring enmity between the Seed of the woman and the devil, and God Himself then and there determining upon the outcome: the Seed of the woman would crush the head of the serpent, but only at a cost, at fatal cost to Himself. The serpent would bruise His heel, the deadly poison would enter into His own being and would kill Him.

Thus you have Calvary already in the Garden of Eden. You have it in God asking Abraham to offer up his only son Isaac, this son whom he so dearly loved, not only to show his love for God but, above all, to show God's love for man. You have it in the brazen serpent, hung up on a piece of wood in the middle of the camp so that whoever looks upon it lives; whoever refuses to look dies. You have it in the history of Israel, God continuing to go after His recalcitrant people, God taking their pain of running away from Him into Himself, so that Isaiah could look and in it all see Golgotha, God laying upon the Lord the iniquities of us all.

But is this really correct, that God in meeting man head on is smashed by man? Man, of course, says that it is all wrong, that is not God, and can prove it. Here, look! Dare Him if He is God! He wants us to believe in Him, He always says. All right, we herewith promise that we will believe in You as our God if You come down from the Cross. And as we insisted all along, He cannot be God; otherwise He wouldn't hang there. In fact, you must wonder now about all the help that He gave to so many others. Was it pure deception? Was it perhaps what some of us insisted all along, that He did what He did by Beelzebub, the chief of the devils? At any rate, it is perfectly clear that if He did help others, He can't help Himself. He forgive sins? He saved others? That's a big laugh when you see it in the light of the fact that Himself He cannot save. He the Son of God? Let God interfere, then, for this His beloved Son if God has the kind of delight in Him that He claims. Wasn't this fair? Wasn't there even something heroic about it to call God so directly into the picture and insist that you will take the consequences by letting this One's blood be upon you and your children? It reminds you of Elijah and the prophets of Baal. That's

67

how Elijah taunted them when their god wouldn't answer because he so obviously was a false god, a god for whom you could prick yourself and writhe and groan and dance and do what you will, he will not answer because he really is not. So the God whose Son this Jesus represented Himself to be wouldn't and couldn't answer either — because He just does not exist.

Let's face it: there is a genuine truth here! You've got to take everything that Jesus claimed about Himself and everything that Jesus demonstrated and hold it up against His Cross. If He was the Son of God, then the Son of God was here dying the most horrible death of a blasphemer. If He saved others, then here is the place where He manifestly cannot save Himself. If He is the One in whom God is well pleased, then here is the place where the good pleasure of God is turned into its opposite. If those hands really reached out and touched lepers and blind and deaf and restored them to full health and use of their faculties, well, now those hands can reach out for nothing except their own pain; and as they clutch, they clutch only upon the great spikes that hold them from touching anyone else. Should not this be proof of something? And on and on you could go, relating every incident of His life to the Cross and letting it throw its ugly shadow across it, from the manger in whose wood you could see the Cross and in whose straw you could catch glimpses of the prickly thorns — all the way through to the raising of Lazarus. If His life was a being about His Father's business, then where does the Cross fit into it all, into the Father's business? That's really the decision with which we are confronted here at the Cross just as surely as were those people who sat there watching. Whatever He is, He also is that on the Cross. If the Cross means that He cannot be the Son of God, then He wasn't the Son

68

of God either under oath, and therefore was guilty of blasphemy. If He was the Son of God indeed, and we cannot help believing it, if for no other reason than for the works' sake, then He is the Son of God also on the Cross, the very same One of whom the angels sang so long ago: "Unto you is born this day in the city of David the Savior, which is Christ the Lord." Now here at the Cross they have to change only the mention of the place, but could sing exactly the same: "Unto you there hangs on the Cross outside Jerusalem the Savior, which is Christ the Lord." Here we have in the sharpest relief the inescapable, always, even now inescapable decision that is inherent in all of our words and deeds and life: "He that is not with Me is against Me."

We maintain that the Word of God reveals His Being here just as surely as that Word reveals His Being all the way through. He is the Son of God, in fact, He is the Word of God made flesh, so that He is the Interpretation of the Word of God. Whoever has seen Him has seen the Father. Now do, as we are told that the watchers at Calvary did: "And sitting down they watched Him there." Sitting down here and looking as intently as we can from this distance, we see Jesus hanging upon the Cross, and we are seeing the Father; otherwise we never see the Father; otherwise we do not know God. What else have we here, then, except God smashed upon the immovable rock of our humanity, God flying to pieces in His efforts to move man! And who ever heard of such a God? Yes, who ever did? But far from being reason for disowning this God, it is His own reason why He is our God. We wouldn't have Him. The Cross is clear enough on that point: The Cross is the judgment which we speak on such a God. We wouldn't listen to Him, and all we have to do here is remember His lament over us: "How often

69

would I have gathered thy children together even as a hen gathereth her chickens under her wings and ye would not!" That is the history of man in His dealings with this God. Man would not, and man will not even to this day!

And make no mistake! All of us are there on Calvary, because there isn't a one of us that cannot find himself there if he is willing to look hard enough and deeply enough. In fact, it may well be that the mixture that goes to make me me is held up here when I see the different types under the Cross. There was the centurion, a very good man, a man interested very much in the right, the highest kind of worldling that you will ever find anywhere. He knows that something went wrong here with Roman justice because, if nothing else, here was a righteous man who was dying. Here we see man, myself, face to face with the heaped-up wrongs of the world and able to do nothing much more than smite upon his breast, and let the wrongs continue to heap up, and regard the wrongs as always done by others, with self having no part in them except to condemn from a distance. There are other soldiers there, the very men who did the crucifying. These were hardened men, like ourselves when we fly in the face of God deliberately, do what we want to do, and make no bones about it, sit only a few feet away from the center of all history and gamble, pass the time, seek our pleasure, even under the Cross, even in church. There are the very religious there, myself therefore at my religious best, the Pharisees and those learned in the Scriptures, masters of their Bibles, respected and ranked in their religion. They were doing their god a service by getting this disturber of the peace out of the way, out of their own way as well as out of the church's way. Christ dare never make Himself central, otherwise the religion of self must always get rid of Him, and if it hang Him upon a Cross to do it. Such always stand there mocking, mocking in the name of God, mocking at the God who is helpless and refuses to do as they demand. And there are disciples there, bewildered by the turn of events, dumb before the sudden onslaught of circumstances over which they had no control, numb because they had trusted in Jesus for deliverance and now He could not even deliver Himself. Yes, we are there, all of me is there and is exposed precisely for what it is; it always is exposed when it is brought beneath the Cross.

And on that that, that I am, God lets Himself go to pieces! How come? The only other alternative would be to break us into pieces, to destroy our rebellion against Him once and for all by destroying us forever in hell. This is the most amazing of all in the God whom we worship in Christ Jesus: He lets Himself be broken utterly rather than break us; He dies rather than destroy us; He gives Himself entirely over to us so that we might have our last full way with Him. Why? There are only two answers: because He loves us and because He is God — and these are after all only one answer, He is the God of love. This is what the crucifixion would make clear for us once and for all: God, the Father of our Lord Jesus Christ, is not the God who stands on His being God, except in love; who claims no majesty except the majesty of His love; who exercises no might except the power of His love; who does not regard us as being there for Him because He regards Himself as being there for us. You will never learn this from your thinking about God, and you will never see this in what you can discover about God outside yourself or in the depths of your soul; you can know this only as you behold the Crucified Christ and already kneel there and confess that this was done for you while you adore Him and say, "My Lord and my God!"

This is how the Cross of Christ is made by God Himself to be wisdom and righteousness and sanctification and redemption. You will notice how this is everything that we need in order to stand before God, and you will also notice that all that we need is thus provided by God Himself in the Cross of Christ. This is why it is God's great deed of love, and this is why when you and I go to glorying, it can never be in ourselves. Now we can glory only in God. What else do we really want? What else do we really need? If God be for us, who can be against us? "If God spared not His own Son but delivered Him up for us all, how shall He not also with Him freely give us all things?" "Who can still condemn us? It is Christ who died," and He is the final Judge in whose hands alone condemnation rests to be meted out, and those hands still bear the scars, because "it is Christ who is risen" and by His scars even "now also makes intercession for us." That's why His arms were stretched so wide on the Cross. He was taking all that we could heap upon Him, and for it He was offering to God the Sacrifice of Himself. Now we see there the arms of God, inviting all who are willing to sit under the Cross beholding: "Come unto Me, all ye that labor and are heavy-laden, and I will give you rest." Our God is God in the Crucified Christ, the God who opened His heart to us and who broke His heart for us and over us. That's why the Cross of Christ is my salvation from God Himself. Amen.

THE SEVEN LAST WORDS

It is not possible for us to reproduce Calvary with everything that took place there, nor is it necessary. Our involvement there does not depend upon how well we can stimulate our imagination or how dramatically we can convey Golgotha's events. We need always keep in mind what is the goal and the purpose of God. As far as He is concerned, He is never after some thrill for us that we will long remember but always and only after faith by which we will always believe. He never attempts to produce wonder and amazement. That's what was wrong with the multitudes that followed Jesus to see the miracles which He performed; God is always attempting to produce that oneness with Jesus Christ whereby we see Him altogether for us and ourselves altogether in Him. God moved into history in the most conclusive way when He sent His Son, made of a woman, made under the Law, to redeem them that were under the Law, that we might receive the adoption of sons, and since that time history can never be the same but can be understood only in the light of His-story, God's mighty deed and intervention for man through Jesus Christ. But God did not do this in order that we might attain to a deeper insight into history and have a better way of filing historical facts and sorting the important from the meaningless; He did it in order that He might be our God in Jesus Christ, our God, who did all that in order that we might know Him as our God right now, the God who never changes and therefore the God who is still in full control and still works His mighty works and still attains His high and holy ends.

This is why the externals of Calvary are largely disregarded. Just how many steps of agony our Lord had

73

to take from Pilate's court to the ugly Place of the Skull; how many blows were necessary to drive each spike home to its eternally destined place through the hands and the feet of the Son of God; how long the Cross was and how deep the hole into which it was set: all this would appeal to our curiosity and thus actually sidetrack the main purpose. In viewing the last hours of Jesus Christ so, we again find a personal escape, the "out" that our flesh is always hungry for, so that it can be entertained instead of edified, invited to a spectacle instead of participating in the revelation of personal guilt. The point that St. Matthew repeatedly makes is the only point of the various props: "All this was done that the Scriptures might be fulfilled." With that we are reminded that regardless of how this may appear to us, with what apparent chance this, that, and the other thing may take place, the Scriptures are being fulfilled. There is no chance; only the working of the predetermined plan of God. Long before, this had been foretold, and only blindness that will not see fails to understand that God is involved here and that God's will over which Jesus prayed in the Garden is being carried out. And if God's will is being done, there is only one thing left for us: to look for our place there under the Cross and continue to look into ourselves for the cause of what there took place and continue to return there again and again, even when Lent is over, in order that we might pray at the place of all grace: "God, be merciful to me, a sinner!"

But why should we attempt to busy ourselves with this for three hours? Our modern life just isn't geared to that sort of participation where there is nothing but listening, a little singing, and then more listening. This is psychologically unsound, and any number of experts will tell you that we can really listen for only about three minutes, not three hours, and then our concentration is gone, and our attention begins to wander. Be that as it may, this modern flesh of ours can well do with some discipline, which means some self-denial, some forcing of its attention instead of having it won, some whipping of it into submission instead of insisting that everything be an indulgence of it. You often wonder just how far you dare go with application, and you know in advance that some of it is far from popular, and some of it opens you to the accusation of being harsh and unloving. But if what we are doing today and any time that we come here is the participation of our faith, the attuning of our ears and our hearts to the Word of God, then we have no choice but to take it as it comes and bow beneath the chastening rod of God in order that He might lift us up to that love of His which does not hesitate to use the rod in order to save us from something far worse. If we have difficulty with these three hours, then let it be as difficult as it will. It cannot be as difficult for us as it was for our Lord, who hung there more than three hours. We think that we don't have to be here in order to be Christian and in order to observe Lent properly; no doubt that is true, just as true as any Christian freedom can make it true. But is there no compulsion in this, that Jesus didn't have to hang there either, that no one could take His life from Him, because He only had power to lay it down and to take it again, that there was nothing compelling Him except His own love for us? It may be that here is where we miss, we who know far more about the Christian faith than we actually believe and are more conversant with some doctrines than we are with God and His Christ. As Christians we are free, and the church has no right to bind us with all sorts of rules and regulations, because Christ has freed us forever.

But it is Christ who has freed us, and it is always only in Christ that we are free, and it is by Christ that we are free only to love, to respond again in love and not under a threat or a must. It is almost like asking: "Must I love God? Must I love Jesus Christ because He loved me?" The real point is that because of Calvary, I again may love God, I again may come back home, I again may be embraced by my heavenly Father in the crucified Redeemer!

This we would make our stated purpose in this Three Hour observance. It was during this time that thick darkness covered the earth, darkness at the brightest hours of the day. All nature grew suddenly still as its Lord entered into that final judgment that would determine the fate of men and that would give ear to the groaning and the travailing of all creatures in their separation from God. We too would make this a quiet time so that we might hear what our Lord has to say to us in offering up Himself as the Sacrifice for our sins. Some would make Calvary a school which we attend and where we hear our great Teacher; this is not enough. We go to Calvary in order that we might behold the Lamb of God taking away the sins of the world, and we listen not primarily to be taught by the greatest of all teachers but to hear our Lord and Savior interpret His suffering and dying for us, Himself telling us what He is doing and why He is doing it, Himself doing what needed to be done over against God for us and at the same time enlightening it all for us so that we might have no false notions with regard to it. God's Word is a lamp unto our feet, we say, and a light unto our path. Christ's Word on Calvary is the lamp unto our feet as they walk the ways of life, our weary, sinful way through life, and the light unto our path into the presence of God.

JESUS' FIRST WORD FROM THE CROSS IS
A PRAYER: "Father, forgive them, for they know
not what they do."

If we know Him at all we expect a prayer. As you
read what is given us of His life, you are repeatedly
made aware of how set He was on working the works
of God and doing His heavenly Father's will. As a result,
time and again you find Him retiring from the active
scene of deed and accomplishment, preaching and healing,
in order that He might be alone with His Father. He
knew that only so could He keep on giving life: only
as He Himself drew again and again on the Source of
all life. Only so could He continue to reveal God: only
as He Himself continued in perfect oneness with God.
Only so could He heal: only as He would bring healing
from Him beneath whose throne flow the waters of eternal
healing. Only so could He speak the Word of God:
only as He Himself listened above the hubbub of life and
the pressures of ongoing demands, listened, with all the
concentration of His praying, for the voice of His Father.
Jesus prayed all His life so that His life was a life of
prayer. "Pray without ceasing," the apostle tells us, and
we wonder how this can even be possible, we who weary
of the effort so soon and whose minds wander before
we can finish a short "Our Father" and who have run
out of needs before we have even well begun. Jesus
demonstrates for us what praying without ceasing means
by living the life whose every breath was prayer, whose
every step was guided by prayer, whose every move was
under the influence of prayer. Even in praying, the most
holy and blessed privilege which is open to us because
we are now the children of God, even here our Lord
Jesus must make good for us, and His perfect praying

must atone for our imperfect praying, and His zeal in praying must make up for our yawns in praying, and His praying without ceasing must somehow stand in the room of our fits and starts at praying if it is all to be acceptable to our Father.

No doubt this is why prayer is so closely related to the Passion and death of our Lord. He needed it for everything that it could do for Him, no question, for He was in all things "tempted like as we are, yet without sin." But in all those things He is acting as our Substitute, taking our place, making good what we had done wrong and fulfilling what we had neglected. This is also why He prayed, not only that I might learn of Jesus Christ to pray but that I might always have the perfect prayer to offer God. "Heavenly Father, my Lord prayed for me His great high-priestly prayer; my Lord prayed for me to the sweating of blood in the Garden; my Lord prayed for me in His very first word from the Cross. Accept this, heavenly Father, as being what He finished for me, completing what I barely begin in praying; always hear that praying of Thy Son whenever I pray, that my praying may be acceptable in Thy sight and may not come colored with my pettinesses and laden with my heavinesses and so earthbound because of my earthlinesses."

"Father, forgive them, for they know not what they do." Many a time Jesus must have prayed for Himself. Even Gethsemane was no isolated incident in His life. When He would spend an entire night in prayer, we may be sure that there were groanings and loud cryings to bring Himself again into oneness with His Father's will, to overcome the keen and bitter disappointment of offering God to men and find them wanting nothing more than bread, to stifle the homesickness which must have

78

welled up within Him again and again as men's lips were so slow to confess faith and to sing the praises of God, so unlike the angels in their ongoing adoration, their beaming countenances, which always reflected only the light which they drew from His Presence. How hungry He must have become at times for a glimpse of the glory that had been His before the foundation of the world, the temple where God Himself is the Light, where God's saints go no more in or out, and where God has wiped away all tears from all eyes that behold Him face to face! What untold misery He had to behold, frightful misery which was altogether of man's own making, terrible misery which man would not let go even when Christ tried to take it from man, unspeakable misery which He could not see without taking it upon Himself, which He could not heal except He Himself should bear our diseases! How He must have prayed for the will and the strength to keep on with it all! How He must have pleaded for that love which would not become discouraged or disgusted but would embrace it all, the worst of it with the best of it, in order that He might present it all holy and spotless unto God!

Now He was in the very midst of the worst that men and devils could do to Him, and as we might expect, if we know Him at all, He prayed. I am confident that I would have prayed as well. Let things get bad enough, and anyone with any spark of memory with regard to the Christian faith sobs out some kind of prayer for help. But here we see how fully Jesus Christ is Savior and Lord for us; His first prayer is not for Himself, for some opium from God whereby His pain would be eased, some superstrength whereby He would be enabled to continue to the bitter end, some closeness to God whereby the awful evidence of hell all about Him might be given some kind of meaning apart from punishment and judgment and torment which threatened to swallow Him up forever. He prayed, not for Himself in the midst of this hell but for those who created this hell for Him. Nor is this merely a pious expression, because He knows that men will surely be punished for doing something like this to Him, something like our prayers with regard to the Fifth Petition. We pray God's forgiveness upon those who hurt us because we are so sure that they will be visited by God, no matter what we pray, because they surely deserve to be visited for something like that. No, it is the sincerest request of what He has the right to request, and He knows it. The Prodigal Son demanded that his father give him what was his, even though it really was not his, and the father gave it to him out of pure love. Jesus here goes to His Father and asks: "Give Me, Father, what is Mine!" And He has the right. That's why He is hanging there, in order that He might have just this right. "Ask of Me," God had said, "and I will give Thee the heathen for Thine inheritance. I will give Thee whatever Thou wilt, for Thou art My beloved Son in whom I am well pleased." "Father, forgive them, for they know not what they do."

Now it is up to us to determine whether we were there prayed for or not. This is a matter of faith, and there can be no faith without judgment. If we would be included in this prayer, we must also be included in its condemnation. God cannot lift us up, not even at or with the Cross, unless we are first made one with the Cross. God cannot make us alive except the Cross have first killed us. Do you want to be prayed for by this first word from the Cross, the prayer which the Father was compelled to answer because of Him who prayed it and because He was offering the very price necessary to

80

enable the Father to do what He was asking? I want nothing more, because only so will I ever be able to appear before God: with the forgiveness of my Lord upon me, prayed for by Him, suffered and died for by Him. All right, He is more than willing to count me in! I am always the unwilling one; I really don't want to be counted in. Ah, but that's not true, we protest. I want nothing more than be under the prayer of Christ, assured of forgiveness from God.

Is it true? Jesus is here praying for all those who did that to Him, so that if I am to be included in the prayer, I must also be included among those who did that to Him. This is the insight into our lives and our daily actions and our little faults, and our snide remarks and our ongoing jealousies and our very meager response to God's love that we claim as our religion; this is the insight whereby all those things are put into their proper perspective and we see them for what they really are in the sight of God. Either I see these things as having brought this woe on Christ, or I am not in this prayer for forgiveness. Either I see these things as nailing the Son of God to the Cross and causing Him this unspeakable agony, or they are not forgiven, however small I may think that they are. Do you want the prayer to apply? Then there is some admitting that you must do and some praying that you must offer up on your own. That's why we are here, and here is the one place where we don't have to be ashamed to own up to it all. Here is the one place where we can finally let down all defenses and barriers and openly confess what we know in our heart and what is revealed by the Cross with regard to our real being. Look again at the Crucified Lord. Hear Him pray for all who did this to Him: "Father, forgive them, for they know not what they do." Then look at all your life, your most recent transgressions and your most distant sin, the things which you did in passing and the things which you did that won't let you pass, and pray in response to this prayer from the Cross:

> My burden in Thy Passion,
> Lord, Thou hast borne for me;
> For it was my transgression
> Which brought this woe on Thee!
> I cast me down before Thee;
> Wrath were my rightful lot.
> Have mercy, I implore Thee;
> Redeemer, spurn me not.

THE SECOND WORD FROM THE CROSS: "Verily, verily, I say unto thee, Today shalt thou be with Me in Paradise."

Be sure that we note that there was no attempt on the part of the Crucified Jesus to accuse anyone here, not even ourselves. This is our first inclination because we are always interested in something less than being totally guilty before God, less than guilty of crucifying His Son and labeling Him a blasphemer who deserved to die. Actually, when Jesus says that they know not what they do, He is therewith presenting their sin before God, the thing that He wants God to forgive them. This was not merely petty ignorance; this was deliberate ignorance, ignorance where there should have been knowledge, because Jesus had given the knowledge; darkness where there should have been light because Jesus had offered that any who followed Him would not walk in darkness but would have the light of life; damnable perversion which is the ultimate in resistance because it is resistance against God, and Jesus had openly shown and perfectly declared God as the God

82

who loves us all. What an indictment of man! They know not what they do! This is the one thing that man is always so sure of, that he knows what he is doing. After all, did he not eat of the fruit of the tree of the knowledge of good and evil? Wasn't his whole quest for knowledge, a quest for knowledge whereby he would be like God? And this is what it all ends up in: Hanging God on the Cross, despising God, rejecting God as God, spitting on God! This is what man is doing in this, that he insists that he knows full well what he is doing!

Do we know what we are doing, even when we sit here beneath the Cross, even when we meditate upon the Passion and death of our Lord Jesus Christ? Do we know what we are doing in our sitting down to eat and to drink and in our rising up to play and in our getting out to work? Do we know what we are doing in our contacts with one another and in what we call our church work and in what is our saving or our spending of our money?

We are so sure that here we are gods and that this has nothing to do with the true and living God and this is something so fully under our control that we can be self-motivated and self-deciding and self-expressing. Well, insist if we will, but here is what comes of it, yesterday when it was done on Calvary and today when it is done in Minneapolis and forever when the same thing can be done only in hell. We will not take God's Word for it, and we will not be directed by God's Word for us, and we will not let God's Word bring Christ into our lives. So we send Him out again to the Cross, the only place for Him if there is no room in our hearts! So we crucify anew the Lord of glory, and we know not what we do because we are sure that we know what we are doing! We know not what we do because we are sure that this is the life and this is the way life must be lived, and you can't sit under a Cross all the time! If the crucified Jesus would not pray for our forgiveness — what would be the judgment? These things done in the Green Tree, and He perished, what would be done in the dry? "Father, forgive them, for they know not what they do."

"My Word shall not return unto Me void," God promised long ago. God, who was so fully involved here on Calvary; God, who here in a special way was keeping promise with His people, not only did He hear Christ's prayer, so that all who see themselves as having anything to do with this hanging on the Cross can be forever sure of their forgiveness, but God also lets this Word of His Son in prayer bring forth immediate fruit for the comfort and encouragement of His people of all time. Two thieves have been crucified with Jesus, and while they were so very much alike in their deeds which brought them to this end, they still were not the same. We are reminded of another word of our Lord where He tells us that one will be taken and the other will be left. Let Him that thinketh he standeth take heed lest he fall. We never take the grace of God for granted; otherwise it is no longer grace to us. The last place we ever presume is Calvary. Prayer, intensive prayer, is called for here, prayer literally out of the depths into which we are thrust here; otherwise we fail to hear the judgment pronounced upon our not knowing what we do, and we will never seek the forgiveness which the crucified Redeemer holds out in His prayers for us.

We are reminded here also that simple punishment as punishment with pain and disgrace is perhaps a deterrent of a sort, but it never brings a man to God. While Jesus was being mocked and spitefully entreated and spit upon, the two who were crucified with Him joined in the sport.

84

Mind you, they knew that they were dying, and still they could persist in their cruelty. Or was it that they were doing it in the name of their religion, that religion which was represented there by the priests and scribes and elders of the people? Was it that they were following their lead and were attempting to find favor with God by going through the same motions as the religious leaders were going through? It is always dangerous in the name of religion to go through somebody's motions only. This was the history of Israel, the people who drew nigh unto God with their lips while they kept their hearts far from God. It is equally dangerous to go through the motions of Christ Lutheran Church without having the heart that must be expressed by the motions. Something like that is always mockery pure and simple, a denial of the Christ, an effort to curry favor with God when we are actually hanging in the same condemnation which is made manifest here in Christ on the Cross, and we justly, because we have deserved it all and worse forever in hell.

One of the two heard the first word of Christ from the Cross and paid attention to it. It worked faith in his heart, a truly great faith, because he turned to his crucified fellow, rebuked him, and confessed his own sin in connection with the rebuke. How many of us would openly and publicly rebuke our partners in sin and then openly and publicly own what terrible sinners we are? We do it in the general confession of sins here in church, and this is where we must be careful that we are not merely going through motions that others have established as being the proper motions. It may well be that we no longer realize what is involved, if an involuntary shudder does not pass through us as we confess that we are poor, miserable sinners, who are by nature sinful and unclean. Maybe we do not see ourselves hanging in the same condemation with Jesus, but we justly because of what our lives have been.

The thief not only rebuked his partner in crime and not only confessed his sorrow at his sin. He turned to Christ, and God help us all to turn to Him in exactly the same way: "Lord," he prayed, "remember me when Thou comest into Thy kingdom." Here was the only believer that there was at the time, the only one who could look at the horror and the misery of that central Cross and pray "Lord," right into the teeth of the most frightful other names that were being called out upon Him, right into the midst of the shame and the scorn that were being heaped upon Him. Here was one who saw what only faith can see, what even faith has difficulty in seeing today, that the Cross was really a throne and that the One hanging there had a kingdom and was entering His kingdom in just this way. And the thief does not presume. He doesn't look for all sorts of advanced guarantees, all sorts of assurances as to whether it will be worth his while, all sorts of questions that must first be answered. He throws himself upon the mercy of Him who prayed for forgiveness, upon those who did that to Him, and asks only to be remembered.

This brought forth the second word from the Cross: "Verily, verily, I say unto thee, Today shalt thou be with Me in Paradise!" He swears an oath that what He is promising will actually be the case. This very day, before the sun goes down upon this scene of unspeakable horror and suffering, with the breaking of the thief's bones, this Lord, to whom he appealed, would take him into Paradise, the hope of every pious Jew, the heaven of God. Nor would the thief have to fear going there into God's presence. He would be there with this One, who was crucified

86

with him, so that if he could hang there with this Jesus and not fear, neither would he have to fear standing where this Crucified One would take him. Only a thief, but one of whom we are sure where he is because of Christ's own dying oath, because he put himself under the prayer for forgiveness. Lord, remember me! This is all that I pray, and in life and death I want no higher assurance than this second word from the Cross. Lord, speak it to me again now, and shout it into my heart when I go to die: "Verily, verily, I say unto thee, Today shalt thou be with Me in Paradise."

THE THIRD WORD FROM THE CROSS: "Woman, behold thy Son! Son, behold thy mother!"

Those that did this to Jesus were prayed for, and whoever of them would could be assured that there was full forgiveness for him. A thief believed, and this forgiveness was spoken personally upon him, even as Christ would speak it personally upon us. But these were not the only ones who were on Calvary. There were some people there who loved Jesus, people who had come to see what the end would be. In this connection we cannot but note that all who had professed love for Jesus were not there. Judas had flung his price of betrayal into the temple when the priests would not assure him of forgiveness that was available also for him. Peter had run off wherever you run to when you've got nothing left to do but weep bitterly, not only because you made a fool of yourself by refusing to be warned, but worst of all, by denying the only One who ever loved you and whom you still really loved for all your denial. The rest of the disciples had gone into that hiding from which they did not emerge until their fears were allayed and their courage restored and their faith renewed into what God Himself created as faith. Their simple attachment to Jesus was not enough for this kind of crisis, and their human love could not stand this kind of strain, and their kind of following was shown up for what it was in their running away into hiding lest they be implicated and end up on a cross of their own.

But where were the others? Though this was done outside the city of Jerualem, it was not done in secret. Where were those who had been healed by Jesus? Where were those who had received their sight, not merely the sight of their eyes but their spiritual sight whereby they confessed Jesus as the Son of God, their Savior? Where were now the praises of those who had been dumb but had been given their speech so that they could again praise God and glorify Him in His Christ? Where were those who had been given their hearing so that they could hear the Word of God, hear this prayer of forgiveness which Jesus prayed from His throne of mercy and hear His assurance that He was able to give a thief who turned to Him in faith? We don't know where they were! Surely many of them must have been in Jerusalem for the feast of the Passover, but they were not at Calvary when their great Benefactor was being put to death. Where were they? Surely they knew that they had not been deceived, no matter what the accusers said. Surely they meant what they said when they confessed Jesus as Lord. But they weren't there, and we can only put the best construction on their absence, because God does not tell us why they were not there. We hope that they did not know. We pray that they were only temporarily confused and their hearts were opened again by the resurrection. We believe that it was no worse with them than it is so often with us, who have received the ultimate in benefits from the Son of God and yet are not always there when His name needs

88

to be confessed and His cause must be represented and sacrifices are demanded. God gives us grace as we attempt to be there now, because we have been absent only too long and too often. We surely would not have been there if we had been alive then, except perhaps to mock, because we demand a religion that gives results on our terms, not a religion which here frowns on human initiative and merely demands faith on God's terms.

But Jesus' mother was there, a few other women, at least two more women, and John, the disciple whom Jesus loved. God had told Mary right from the start that it would be no easy thing to be the mother of His Son, and we who want to be included in Jesus' word that all are His mother and brothers and sisters who believe in Him had better remember that as well. Simeon had prophesied the sword that would pierce Mary's soul, and there is bound to be a sword piercing our souls as well. We cannot have this Son of God without a gaping wound to our souls, our egos, this last part of us that we want to surrender. It must always be with us something as it was with Mary, the mother of our Lord.

Surely part of the sword that pierced her soul here was the shame and the agony of her Son whom she loved very dearly, good mother that she had been all His life. She couldn't stroke His brow, give Him a drink, or wipe the mess from His face. She couldn't even hold His hand and press it against her heart from which it had come. All she could do is stand there and weep and let her mother's heart break and sob out her inward WHY to God in stunned and silent unbelief at what was taking place. Never, we say, was a mother subjected to something like this without being able to do at least something about it. Wouldn't Jesus regard her, He who had been so obedient unto her all His days, He who had been the only perfect Son in every sense of the word?

He regards her indeed, and we are at first inclined to say that He regards her in a most wonderful way. He provides for her like any good son would, by turning her over to the loving care of the disciple whom He loved, the disciple that He could trust to do all for His mother that could and should be done. But this is just a little sentimental on our part, and we miss everything on Calvary if we do not yet know that there is more than mere sentiment involved there. Jesus, the Son of God, is suffering and dying for all men. He has taken upon Himself the sins of the whole world, and it is this that He is working out. This is the mightiest battle that will ever be fought anywhere, and every man who lives is involved in it. Victory had better be the outcome, or we are doomed. Jesus Christ had better accomplish here what He set out to do, or we are damned.

Well, then, what about His mother and the disciple that He loved? Part of the sword that here pierced Mary's soul was of her own making, but part of it was of her Son's making, and this was the major part. Mary was no longer to regard herself merely as mother of this wonderful Son. She had to move over here with the rest of us if her Son was to save her. She had to stand over there with the calloused and gambling soldiers so that the first word from the Cross could fall in forgiveness upon her sins, because she did not know what she was doing any more than we do. She had to establish the same contact with Jesus that the thief had established, so that she could cry out that she had deserved that condemnation and could ask for nothing more, mother or not, than to be remembered by this her Son when He entered His kingdom, into which she had no

90

automatic entrance. This is always the problem that we have with God. He asks us to do something, and then we think we should be rewarded for it, while He insists that at best we are always only unprofitable servants. He asks Mary to be the mother of the Christ, and then lets her know that the blessing was in being what He had asked her to be and the reward was in His grace which condescended to use her for His highest purposes. And in the end she has to stand there like any other and look for the same thing from this Jesus as anyone else.

Woman, behold thy son! With that the mother relationship is brought to an end, and Mary is to become what everyone of us must become if we would be blessed by Jesus: a simple believer; someone with no claim but the claim of the grace which Jesus was here offering to thieves and gamblers and mockers and spitters. Mary's heart had to be torn from her mother status in order that she might be blessed by being remembered by Christ when He would come into His kingdom.

This is a hard saying as long as we still do not believe and do not know the heights to which Christ elevates us when He breaks every natural connection with us in order that He might be the Savior of sinners. We give Him nothing; He gives Himself to us and for us. He is first and always about the Father's business, not Mary's business or what is our human business. And that business is salvation for us, the Cross as the open gateway to heaven for us, the sword through our hearts in order that we might finally and fully die to everything except this Jesus, who would be King and Lord even as He is perfect Savior. Only so do we see ourselves aright. Only so do we see one another aright as the mothers and brothers and sisters of our Lord.

THE FOURTH WORD: "My God, My God, why hast Thou forsaken Me?"

The sacred narrative is not interested in giving us a running account of what took place at Calvary because it would neither serve a remote and speculative interest nor satisfy an idle curiosity. It is for faith, and so it speaks only for the edifying of faith and only to the understanding and the comprehension of faith. And faith knows that there is an awful mystery here, because faith believes that here God has gone to the depths for man; here the Innocent One suffers for the guilty, and here the Sinless One is the archtransgressor, for on Him was laid the iniquity of us all. Here is where justice and mercy are met together, and justice can be the justice of God because in mercy sin is taken seriously, so seriously that mercy must die in order to be the mercy of God. Behold, ye ends of the earth, this is your God upon the Cross extended, and He looks more like the utter rejection of everything that you regard as good and sacred and even decent. "Come and see," He must lament, "was there ever sorrow like unto My sorrow?" And there is reason why He should be known as the Man of sorrows of whom faith does not hesitate to declare that He is the God of sorrows.

But nature cannot bear to look, because it is itself involved. St. Paul reminds us that all nature groans and travails together until now, waiting for the redemption of the sons of God. God's world is involved in man, and so it partakes of the misery which man has created, and every step of the sinner brings forth a groan from all creation, which must remain true to its nature, true to its God. Here on Calvary everyone must take his place and play his shameful part out to the bitter end and show his sin for what it is as the despising of God. Nature cannot remain

92

unmoved, and at high noon the sun is darkened for three hours. Was it an eclipse? Was it something else that our scientific age knows how to explain? It still does not explain God away, the God who is the Causer of the causes and the God who is the Supporter of that which supports man. Darkness covers the earth at earth's brightest, and suddenly everything has become hushed and still. It is night while it is high day, and we cannot but be reminded of the end of all things, when the sun will lose its light and the moon and the stars will not be able to take their place. It is the time of intensest judgment, and the whole world is before the tribunal of the Almighty. Jesus has entered into the holiest of holies, the very presence of God, and He has gone in all alone where no eye can penetrate, all alone except for our sin. He hangs there before God guilty with every guilt which sinful man ever heaped up before his Maker. And the sun hides its face; the morning stars quit singing together; the angels strain at the will of their God in order to fly to their Lord's help; the birds make no twittering; the cattle and beasts on a thousand hills to which God lays claim silently and dutifully retire before the hand of their Maker. There is one place where God is, on Calvary, and all the rest of the world must know what it is like to be without God. The real Light of the world is being extinguished: why should man yet see?

What was this on the part of nature? Participation with its Lord or further judgment upon Him? No doubt both: participation because all things were made by Him and all things are upheld by Him. How can He perish, and what He has made and what He upholds not be moved? But it is above all further judgment. This earth which man ruined by his fall is no longer the friend of man. In sweat and toil he must work it to compel it to give forth its fruits for his needs. But because of his sin

93

it is all that he knows as home. He has become of the earth, earthy. Take this away from him, and he has nothing left, though he probe space to its outmost bounds and though he make a place for himself on the moon. And so he takes comfort in the solid ground under his feet and the accustomed sounds in the air about him and in the sight and the smell of its trees and flowers. Now Jesus is deprived also of this, so that He is left altogether without support of any kind. It reminds us of His temptation in the wilderness (perhaps someone should study Calvary altogether in the light of the threefold temptation). He must do battle alone with none to help Him, with no lilies to speak to Him of the lavish care of His heavenly Father and no birds flying over His head to remind Him that His Father knows His needs and richly supplies them.

He is alone, far more alone than we can even begin to realize, because out of the dark we now hear the agonizing cry of Him who is the very Son of God: "My God, My God, why hast Thou forsaken Me?" We may listen, but we do not hear aright unless we hear this as the cry of Him who bore our griefs and carried our sorrows, who was wounded for our transgressions and bruised for our iniquities, so that it was the chastisement of our peace that was upon Him in order that by His stripes we might be healed. What does it mean? It means that there is no possible condition of life, no real or imaginary sorrow, no shattering grief and no excruciating pain, no sudden onslaught of suffering, and no day-by-day wasting away and only waiting for the next overwhelming wave of unbearable agony, nothing whatever in which a man can ever again be alone. This is the sum total of all the cries that filter through clenched teeth or tightly closed doors, the strange shrieks that come from the places of care for the mentally ill, the heavy breathing of the dying who will not

94

die, the loud groans of the dead who cannot die, the convulsive sobs of the widows over the coffins to be closed for the last time, the numbed response of our own aching hearts when they are so crushed that all they can do is bleed. Here is the One who came over to our side, really came over so that He not only knows but also bears. He looks with sorrowful eyes into the eyes of sorrow, and He winces with pain at every new start of the sufferer, and he takes into His great heart this mystery of misery which is human life and which we shall never be able to understand, much less manage. Here He took it all and held it out before His God, and — and what? There was no answer, any more than there is an answer when we are in our most desperate straits. If only there were an answer, if only this all did not appear utterly senseless, it could still be borne. But when it is so dark that you cannot see even the next step or a hand to crush or help you before your eyes; when the heaven is as silent as the tomb you are heading for and thereby seems to give its own full approval to all that you must bear, then we can only cry out our fearful *Why* because we know that we are forsaken of God.

But look, even though it is so dark about Calvary. The looking here requires the eyes of faith anyway. Mystery unfathomable that we have here, it is also the most enduring comfort that our Lord can give us. The mystery is in this that He should be forsaken of God, He who claimed absolute oneness with the Father. If you look now and see Him, do you also now see the Father? Is this the One who already was before Abraham? Is this the One who is the Resurrection and the Life, so that if a man lives and believes in Him he shall never die? Is this the Way, the Truth, and the Life, so that only by Him does a man come to the Father? Listen again: "My God, My God, why hast Thou forsaken Me?" This much we must hear: God takes sin seriously, so seriously that He forsakes His Son who was made to be sin for us. And Jesus Christ was truly made to be sin for us; otherwise He would never have been forsaken of God. If He can manage this, we have a perfect Savior. If He is for us here, He will be for us all the way through.

But there is further comfort here for us. This was no make-believe coming to us by the Son of God, a kind of play-acting, the Son of God going only so far with us and then, when things reach their unbearable worst for us, turning back to His throne of glory. He went all the way down, into the deepest depths of our tragedies, into the bottomless pit where life itself becomes meaningless. He too must cry out His *why* as do we almost daily, and He too must know what it means to be left alone, all alone, so alone that you cannot see or count on God's hand, which is the support of all that there is. As a result, this can never again be our cry, for in this darkness of God-forsakeness, we now have a companion, the Friend who sticketh closer than a brother. He tied Himself to me for good or ill, and here is the depth of the ill to which He goes for me and with me. Here is His hell that He might cry my cry to God and I might never cry it again, because this One is with me forever, even unto the end of the world. Now there is always a hand that I can grasp, though I cannot see it for the dark, and I know whose it is and why it is there because by faith I can still feel the scar of the nail. Now there is always One who knows far better than I do and One to whom I can turn because He is always there and He is there for me, so that though I walk through the last dark, the valley of the shadow of death, I need fear no evil. This One is there for me, waiting to take me on through into the light of God's new day.

But there is something else here that we dare not over-look. When Jesus cries out His *why* of God-forsakeness, He shows us the way here, the only way by which we can be kept from despair. We usually make our cries loud enough for others to hear us. We want witnesses to the fact that God has forsaken us, as though we had summoned God before our tribunal and could accuse Him of injustice. Look, He who promised: I will never leave thee nor forsake thee, He has forsaken me! Why, Why, Why? And there is no answer; indeed, there cannot be, because we have withdrawn ourselves from God. This Jesus refused to do, even when there was every reason why He should and the hell about Him insisted that God had nothing to do with Him any more and the devil at His side kept whispering to come down from the Cross in order that He might again be with God. Jesus Christ, even here, did as He always had done. He turned to God Himself and made His appeal, not about God having forsaken Him but to the God who could not possibly forsake Him, though everything said that He did. This is basic to our faith, Jesus still holds to God when there is no reason left why He should, and Jesus cries to God when the heavens are so dark that He cannot see God or any trace of Him. My God, why hast Thou forsaken Me? He is not crying out a curse or an accusation. He is not appealing to man or the devil. He is not looking around for reason in himself or evidence for God. He cries directly to God Himself, the God with whom He is here involved, the very God who so apparently won't have anything more to do with Him.

It is very dark on Calvary now, but because Jesus is there, from this dark we draw our single light, the only light that will never go out for us. God is there, He is always there, and because of this Jesus Christ He is always

97

there for you: Only dare it; no matter what, throw yourself upon Him, and you will find that underneath are the everlasting arms and spread over you are the wings of mercy — that's really why it is so dark. God's hand gets between you and everything else, but only in order to caress your fevered brow and strengthen your weak hand and bear you up to the glory where you will be forever face to face with your God. This is what faith hears when it listens in the dark and knows what is involved when Jesus cries out: "My God, My God, why hast Thou forsaken Me?"

THE FIFTH WORD FROM THE CROSS: "I thirst!"

The words come now in quick succession because hell has been endured, the cup which the Father had given the Son to drink was all but empty. The Scriptures still needed to be fulfilled on certain matters, to us perhaps unimportant, but eternally important to God. One of the Psalms reminds us that this mighty Savior would drink of the brook in the way. He is shown in His great battle on man's behalf. As the enemy is put to flight, He pursues, and in order to summon His last full strength and to draw upon all His resources He stoops in the way for a drink. And out of the darkness of Calvary we hear Jesus cry, "I thirst." This is in order that the Scriptures might be fulfilled. So often this sounds as though there had been a script written in advance, and Jesus was here following the script like an actor in a drama. There was that, to be sure, but not in the sense in which we might imagine. It was not a kind of make-believe like all play-acting. The script was written in advance because God's promises are of old. But Jesus was really everything that had been promised of old, so that you can look at His whole life and all

His doing, and you will find no detail in which He is not the promised Messiah. Thus He fulfilled the Scriptures because they testified of Him from the beginning. He cried out, "I thirst!" because it was of just this very suffering thirst on the Cross that the Scriptures spoke, even though men read the passage with the veil over their hearts and do not even know that it is speaking about this Christ. In other words, we are reminded again that you read your Bible in order to know Christ, the Son of God, your Savior. The Old Testament testifies of Him, and the New Testament proclaims Him, so that if we miss Him we have missed everything.

Thus He did not cry out, "I thirst!" because that was the proper line that should be read. He so cried out because He suffered agonizing thirst; but now we look back, and we know what the Scriptures were talking about when they so spoke of this thirst long before. What does this mean for us? Surely we are reminded once more that we are at the place of unbelievable suffering, inhuman torture, and depths of agony that we cannot even fathom. For all of our *whys,* we could never cry out as Jesus did here. No one can except the damned in hell. The damned in hell! And Dives pleaded that Abraham would send Lazarus to dip his finger in water and let one drop from it fall upon his tongue, for he was in terrible torment in this flame. Could Jesus really have suffered hell torment and not have suffered thirst? Listen again as He cries out, "I thirst!" You know where He has been, and you know where you should have gone; but because He suffered even this thirst for you, He was able to carry off the doors and even the hinges of hell, so that it can never hold any who belong to Him.

But this cry tells us that He is true man as well.

So true, we say, don't we have the evidence of that all around, from His lying in the manger through His hot and dusty walk through life? We do indeed, but being what we are, we do not always hold to what is offered us by God. As a result, when our going gets rough and someone tries to tell us of the Christ who is with us in all of it, and not only makes it all bearable but also gives it reason and purpose, we are apt to shrug it off in order to sit alone with our grief and wallow in our misery. And if that one in all love persists in pointing us to the Christ who sticketh closer than a brother and who knows what we are involved in because He was involved in even worse, we are inclined to dispute that; if not out loud, then at least in the silence of our unbelief. We are always tempted to look at Christ as something less than true man, bone of our bone and flesh of our flesh. We always like to think that He had resources to draw on that are not available to us and thereby discount His ability to endure and see no relation between what we are going through and what He suffered. This is why we have certain reservations even with regard to His being forsaken of God. It just cannot be, not in any real sense of the word in which I must experience God-forsakenness. There was always the hidden support there; there was always the certainty that He was the Son of God and could come down from the Cross.

This is not true, but it is one of those last and clever devices of the devil by which he would bring us to persist in doubt until it becomes unbelief. This was the very temptation by which the devil attempted to bring Christ under his command, the temptation to doubt that He was the Son of God because He was as bound as we are. "If Thou be the Son of God, command that these stones be made bread." Jesus was hungry, hungrier than we

100

ever get. This shouldn't be for the Son of God. Here take this out if you are the Son of God. What we like to think of as the area of His greatest strength the devil uses as the point of his attack. This is how he always got man, and gets man to this day, by attacking man in his strength. Jesus, however, will have none of it, and He persists, not by adducing any proof that He is the Son of God and thereby doing exactly what the devil wanted, but by holding on in faith, the only proper relation with God that there is. Hence the response which defeats Satan: "Man shall not live by bread alone but by every word that proceeds out of the mouth of God." Jesus Christ was true man, and as such He used no more than we have: faith by which He could overcome, faith by which we can also overcome.

But if we know anything at all from direct and personal experience, it surely must be this that the devil never gives up, but comes back again and again, pounding away at us until he is able to make a breach in the wall of our defense. He tries this also with Jesus. In the wilderness it was an appeal to Jesus' hunger; here on Calvary it is an appeal to Jesus' thirst. In both instances, Jesus had every right to doubt that He was the Son of God under these circumstances, and who would have blamed Him if He had spoken the word by which His senses would again have something to hold to, something besides bare faith. He has every reason to think that He is forsaken of God, every reason to take seriously, just as seriously as the devil can make a man take anything, that if He is the Son of God He should come down from the cross, that God has forsaken Him only because He hangs there; that this agonizing thirst shows that His body is being left to perish in hell. Do something, something comparable to making bread out of stones or jumping down from the temple or bowing down and worshiping the devil, so that all the kingdoms of the world and the glory of them which quenches thirst may be yours.

And Jesus cries out, "I thirst!" He is true man for man's sake, and He will overcome as man in order that He might overcome for man. Can He be the Son of God? He is not even served as a common criminal with some rights to humanitarian treatment. They give Him vinegar to drink but not without pointing to His shame and not without using it as an occasion for more mockery. Let's see if Elias will come and take Him down from the Cross! And everyone had a good laugh because He had helped others and now could not quench His own thirst. He has claimed to be the Son of God! That's a good one, the Son of God who must cry out, "I thirst!"

Yes, Son of God, who cries out, "I thirst!" Let it be a source of temptation from the devil, and let it be a reason of mockery from those who know everything about God and what God must do and how God must be and act! Faith bows very low here because this is the Son of God, its Savior. Even in His thirst He remained true to His purposes and faithful to God's will. He would not use means not available to us whom He was championing and saving. He will not be anything but a genuine Savior of them that believe. He is the Son of God though He cries out, "I thirst!" even because He so cries out. Flesh of my flesh, bone of my bones, He overcame the devil, who overcomes me by appealing to my needs, my hungers, and my thirsts. "I thirst," and as they give Him vinegar to drink, I know that by Him I can live by every word that proceeds out of the mouth of God. I live because He suffered thirst.

102

THE SIXTH WORD FROM THE CROSS: "It is finished!"

"Lo, I am come to do Thy will, O My God!" This
was the interpretation which Jesus gave to His own life,
so that if you want to ask with regard to any part of it
why He did this or that and said such and such, there
is the answer. "I am come to finish His work," to bring
to completion what is the work of God and what only
God can do, to make an accomplished fact what God
has already foreknown. This is why He is the Word
of God. We remember that the creation story tells us
God said, "Let there be," and there was. Let there be
light, and there was light. God thought it, and God willed
it, and God spoke it. That's how this world came into
being. In the counsels of eternity God thought out and
planned our salvation. This is the love of God that He
willed sinners to be saved. But here was something which
He could not merely speak into being. Here was something that God had to work into being because He is God.
It is not as simple for Him as for us, because He is God
and whatever He says actually is. We tell someone that
we forgive him, but this is quite superficial, and we might
hold all sorts of reservations with regard to the forgiveness
and the one forgiven. But God works out what He says,
and what He declares is reality. When therefore He
forgives, there must be a very real taking away of the
sin, and the only way it can be taken away is if God
takes it into Himself. The other alternative would be
to damn it forever in hell so that it would no more rise
up in the sight of God. But God would not damn us.
This is why Jesus came, to fashion forgiveness so that it
would be reality and not merely word in our sense of
the word. This, then, is Christ doing the will of God,

103

for this is the will of God, even our salvation. This is Christ working the work of God and bringing it all to completion in order that there might be a finished redemption for us.

We need think of only one passage here. God says, "I have removed your sins from Me as far as the East is from the West, and I remember them against you no more." But this is God who speaks, the God who is all-knowing, the God who cannot possibly forget. The only way this promise is possible for God is if He does something with our sins that really removes them as far as the East is from the West, if He really does something with our sins that causes them to exist no longer, and thus His mind can be wiped clean of them, and the omniscience of God cannot even remember them, so fully are they done away. This is what Jesus came to do, and this was the God-given purpose that ran through all of His life. We hear it already at Bethlehem as we are told that to us is born the Savior, Christ the Lord. We see it at His circumcision, where He shed His first blood in order that His name might properly be called Jesus, for He would save His people from their sins. We hear it from the 12-year-old Boy: "Wist ye not that I must be about My Father's business?" We hear it in His reproach of His enemies as He tells them that He is come to seek and to save that which was lost. We hear it in His invitation "Come unto Me, all ye that labor and are heavy-laden, and I will give you rest." We see it in His prayer of the bloody sweat in Gethsemane, His bearing of the Cross, His hanging upon the accursed tree, His being forsaken of God, His agonizing thirst. Here is the Savior of sinners! Here is the working of the work of God and the completing of God's work, for God so loved the world that He gave His only-begotten Son that

whosoever believeth in Him should not perish but have
everlasting life.

Now Jesus cries out with a loud voice, "It is finished!"
It is almost as if He needed that drink in order that
He might so cry out and that He might cry out in the
loudest possible voice. The very loudness of the cry
impressed the centurion, so much so that he smote upon
his breast and confessed Jesus as a righteous man and
the Son of God. This was one cry that Jesus wanted
everyone to hear, and He was still able to cry out with
a loud voice. The loudness tells us very plainly that He
Himself finished His work, and no one was shoving Him
into an end that was not part of the whole purpose of
His coming. No man was taking His life from Him.
He had power to lay it down, and He had power to
take it again. So He cried out with a loud voice: "It is
finished, it is completed!"

To whom was He so crying out? Surely to His Father
who had sent Him into the world, into this far place
from home, in order that He might work the works of
God. He was telling His Father that as He looked it
all over from His vantage point on the Cross He could
see that His mission had been accomplished. He was
now ready to come home.

Surely He was shouting this into the teeth of the
devil, who had had his last desperate go at Christ in His
great thirst. "Satan, you are overcome, because you
have no part in Me, and you have nothing more to do
with those who belong to Me!"

Surely, He was shouting with a loud voice so that
all who during the long past of God's covenant dealings
with Israel, those who believed God, would hear and re-
joice. This was what Abraham already longed to see,

105

and he saw it and rejoiced to see Christ's day in faith and was glad. This is what David sang of so longingly in his beautiful psalms, David, who needed this special assurance of total forgiveness because of his most grievous sin. This is what old Simeon saw already in the Babe, for God had permitted him to see the salvation which God had prepared before the face of all people, a Light to lighten the Gentiles and the Glory of God's people Israel. Now it was all completed, and their faith had not been made ashamed.

Surely He wanted those to hear it who stood there at the Cross and who mocked Him and spit upon Him and yowled so loud that they did not hear anything that they did not want to hear. But Jesus cried with such a loud voice that they had to hear, hear at least enough to sow the seed for Peter's sermon on Pentecost and to know not only that they killed the Prince of Life but also that "neither is there salvation in any other, for there is none other name under heaven given among men whereby we must be saved," because He could cry out, "It is finished!"

Surely, then, He also wanted us to hear and believe. He had come to be our Way to God. It is finished, the Way is open, and whatever of sin and disobedience clogged the way and presented barriers to God beyond our overcoming are now cleared away, because it is finished and He is the Way, so that we can now come to the Father by Him. He is the Truth because now this is a faithful saying and worthy of all acceptation, that Christ Jesus came into the world to save sinners, of whom I am chief. He is the Life because He took all of our sinful life into Himself and died its deserved death of curse on the Cross so that we might get it back from Him as eternal life,

life of the restored relation with God, life that is His own great gift to us.

"It is finished!" Now whoever would doubt his personal salvation calls this word of the dying Christ into question. Now whoever lets sin plague him beyond what is right does not take this work of Christ seriously. Now whoever lives his life in fear and anxiety is living as though this word of Christ were a lie, as though there is still something left that we must do, as though something can yet separate us from the love of God which is in Christ Jesus, our Lord. "It is finished!" With that the great veil in the temple tore from top to bottom, and man, not merely His representative, but man himself, as man is in himself, can go into the Holy of Holies, into the very presence of God. Never let this loud cry of your Savior die in your heart. Whatever may come upon you, let it echo from your faith as you meet life and death with this cry from the Cross: "It is finished!"

THE SEVENTH WORD FROM THE CROSS: "Father, into Thy hands I commend My spirit!"

Here is the word of final comfort for us, the final interpretation of the Cross and the suffering and dying of our Lord Jesus Christ. There is much more here than we can possibly fathom. But if we will call on faith to listen well, it can be greatly edified. It can see heaven opened to it and know the source of power and strength to endure, to live, and to die.

For one thing, be sure that faith notes that Jesus here again calls God Father. He is back in the bosom of the Father and is not estranged from the Father, so that He can only cry out to God. This can mean only one thing: God Himself agreed with the previous cry. God

107

Himself is telling us here that it is all finished indeed and the time of man's forsakenness is over because His guilt is pardoned and there is double grace for all his iniquity. Jesus had gone all alone into the holiest of the holies. He had been in the presence of God. It was dark, and He was under the full wrath of God, the wrath of God as it was visited upon all sin. This was Christ's hell for us, and only Christ's faith kept Him from perishing in the final despair that would have made it eternal hell of God-forsakenness for Him and equally hell of separation from God for us. But He had paid the price. God did not reject His work but declared it the completion of all that was the purpose of God in the sending of His Son. God did not remain the God veiled in wrath as He visited the curse upon all sin in His own Son. Jesus is now going home, back to the bosom of the Father, where He had been from all eternity. He could again pray to His Father. That's why this same Jesus always urges us to pray, "Our Father who art in heaven." After the dark of Calvary there isn't a person in the world who cannot so pray if he will pray through the Jesus who prayed, "Father, into Thy hands I commend My spirit."

Be sure also that you find here faith's full and final vindication by God Himself. What made the dark of Calvary so awful? Jesus' cry tells us. He was forsaken of God. He looked about for His Father, and His Father had withdrawn Himself. He reached out for His Father's hand, and His Father's hand only reached out to smite Him and push Him away from His holy presence. But Jesus still clung to God in faith and still held to His promises as He cried out, "My God" and "Why hast Thou forsaken Me?" He couldn't see the hand, but it had to be there. He could only feel it in wrath, but it was still the hand of His God; God, who was still "Thou" to Jesus; God, to whom Jesus appealed when His only complaint was that God was not there. But only for a moment does God deal so with His children, specially with His Son. Only for a moment does God hide Himself in order that He might visit us with loving-kindness and tender mercy forever and thus succor us. This is the interval of faith, when faith holds on because it is faith in God, even though it gets as dark and difficult as Calvary.

But hang on it not only must, but hang on it also may. God's hand is still the hand of the merciful Father, and the blow from His hand is only to kill the sin which still besets and plagues us, and the shadow is only the hand of God reaching out to help. This is why Jesus could pray after the hell of God-forsakenness: "Father, into Thy hands I commend My spirit." The hands of God were not evident, but when Jesus appealed to My God and threw it all on Him with the THOU, the hands were there and ready to receive everything that Jesus committed to them. "I will never leave thee nor forsake thee," God promises. Dare to believe Him as Jesus did out of the dark, and the hands will be there to receive your spirit also.

"Learn of Jesus Christ to die." That's how the hymn encourages us. Better if we would sing: Now in Jesus Christ I die. His death was my death because my sin had become His sin. Now there is no sin in me as I am in Christ, because it is all finished. Now there is no death for me because there on the Cross is my death. Well, then, what is this that we call death? What is this coffin-choosing and gravedigging and cemetery-lot buying? All it is now is a commending of our spirits into the hands of the Father, putting them where they are safe even now and the only place where they are safe even now. It is where Christ broke the path for me that I commend my spirit into the hands of the Father. So my Lord did in order that He might die for me and prepare a place in those hands for my spirit.

And then Jesus died, better, He gave up the ghost. By His own deed and action He confronted the last enemy, death, in order that He might be the death of death, even as He became the sin of sin and the curse of all curse. He died for me in order that I might never die, in order that I might have God always as my Father in Christ. He died for all that they which live should not henceforth live unto themselves but unto this Christ, who died for them and rose again. Whether therefore we live, we live unto the Lord; whether we die, we die unto the Lord. Whether therefore we live or die, we are the Lord's. He bought us and at what a price! But He did go through with it, we are the bought ones, we are the redeemed of God by Christ Jesus. Go in peace! Die in peace! In all of your going and finally in your dying there is nothing but peace because Jesus has prepared your real resting place forever. Take it as you pray with Him: Father, into Thy hands I commend my spirit, for Thou hast redeemed me, Lord God of hosts. Peace in the hands of God. Peace through the scarred hands of Christ. This is the meaning of Calvary and the Cross of Christ, the meaning which Christ Crucified Himself gives it as He speaks seven times to interpret it all for faith and then dies, then commends His spirit into the hands of His Father. Amen.

CHRIST'S RESURRECTION
The Breach in the Wall of Time

Mark 16:1-8

Happy Easter! Blessed Easter! Joyous Easter! Surely something like this must be the theme of this great day, and God knows that in a world like ours and in a life like this we can use all the happiness and all the blessedness and all the joy that any day can give us. Let's be sure then that we do not miss the boat and pass up this ideal opportunity for goading our dullard spirits into a response that they do not too often make; for coaxing our emotions into a participation that will make our hearts sing in echo to the theme of this glorious Easter morning. Push the depressing thoughts aside now for the moment, and concentrate solely and only upon the bright and the gay thoughts. Forget the cemetery for a while, the place where you laid your loved one not too long ago and so the place where you had to buy a lot for your own lying only too soon. Turn away from the old family sores that just have not healed over the years but have festered between you and your close ones until it is hard to speak even a civil word any more to each other. Deliberately close your eyes to the neighbor, the ex-friend, the not-distant-enough relative, who cause you to boil within yourself every time you remember what they have done to you and what they think of you. Yes, tomorrow is Monday with all the same old grind and grief again, but today is Easter Sunday. Next week you pay the bills, and all the old fretting and striving begins once more, perhaps even more than usual because of the preparations for this day. But let's not spoil it all; at least get whatever good out of it that we can and make some of these expenditures worthwhile. All right? Everybody all set, then? Now here we go!

If this is what it all means and if this is the kind of preparation that has gone into your coming, then we had better observe a brief pause here and now and let those depart who have come that way and for that purpose. We want everyone to know that if nowhere else in the world, you can still find honesty here in this church. And with all the honesty that we can possibly express and before you have wasted the entire morning we would tell you that this is not what we are going to attempt. This is precisely what has brought the church into disrepute with the honest seekers that are left. The false seekers have given them this wrong impression, that the church would help us stimulate certain moods in ourselves and captivate us with a type of self-hypnosis. This is nothing else than hiding from reality and firing up the imagination into seeing what is not there and listening to old wives' tales that cannot do anything but offend those who want to live and are looking for the resources that will make for a life that is genuine and realistic and enduring. If the church has nothing to say about reality, then it had better be quiet and let the superior media of our day do the entertaining and the providing of escapes. If the church is there for the creation of moods only, Christmas mood and Easter mood, then it is going about this all wrong, and for all the high attendances it is being swept aside by the much more aggressive and meaningful materialism of secularistic America and Communistic Russia. There are people and powers abroad today who want nothing to do with dreams and who will not hesitate ruthlessly to puncture every dream with which they come into contact. Therefore if the church is helping people spin dreams, it is offering

112

opium to the people and is merely pandering to what is the lowest in man; his refusal to live life as life is. Drug addiction, alcoholism, churchgoing then all belong in the same class, especially on Easter.

Easter maintains, when it is given a chance to maintain what God says, that it is the sole reality, the great reality on which every silly dream shatters and every false hope founders and every escape goes to pieces. Easter insists that it is life, and without it you still do not live. Easter declares that you are running away from God into a self-chosen destiny of desperation if Easter is this one day only and not all your days. Easter will plainly tell you that you never heard its message, and you don't deserve hearing it, if you associate it merely with a mood and if you want to use it merely to exhilarate your feelings for the moment and be able to close your eyes to the bitternesses and the heartaches of life, your own and those of others. The day's theme has to do with such things as death, real death, which holds you in its grip and which day by day is more fully exercising its claim upon you. The day takes you to a tomb as the goal of life, and we had better not look in too closely, or we shall be looking not merely into the place where they laid Him but into the place where they will lay us. The day's account has to do with bitter tears, disappointed hopes, fear that borders on sheer panic. The day, in other words, is extraordinarily realistic and takes hold of things where man actually is and tears aside every pretense with which man would hide his nakedness and reveals the ulcers on his fondest hopes and the gaping wounds in what he is so sure is his health. The day is the most dangerous day of the year, and only the brave had better take it seriously, because it surely will smash you unless it refuses to speak to you or you refuse to let it speak. Then preen yourself under whatever pur-

113

chased finery you would still kid yourself with and smell
your lilies and fool yourself into believing that this world
is a great flower garden and your life a stroll through the
park that will end with a permanent stay in an even more
glorious park. Then by no means let the day change
a thing, and keep your old schedules, and continue in your
own old rounds, and look for the same old joys, and don't
miss a single show. But know that you are keeping your
appointment equally with death, and know that there will
be no TV in the grave and no pockets in your shroud and
no final escape from the voice of God, whose voice you
are daily trying to escape, whose voice you want to escape
especially at Easter. May God speak His Easter to us as
we consider

Christ's Resurrection the Breach in the Wall of Time

No doubt some will think this a pretty rough beginning, especially for a wonderful day like this. But is it
really? However vigorously you shook your youngsters
this morning to wake them up and however threatening
you made your voice sound in order to get them out of
bed, the real love of your heart was conveyed by your
purpose: You didn't want them to miss any of the glories
of the day, especially this day. You know that being awake
in the day is much better than being asleep. If that were
not true, then your love would have prevented them from
being born to begin with, or being born, your love would
feed them sleeping pills because the fewer hours they
would be awake, the better. Not one of us that doesn't
need this from God; not one of us that doesn't need to
be shaken, however roughly, lest we doze on with our
sleeping world and let its reactions to God become decisive
for our faith. It is so easy for us to make this all some-

114

thing downy and cozy that you want to snuggle down into, asking nothing more than that someone fluff our pillows and straighten out our wrinkled sheets. In that way the church becomes a glorified resthome for those who want to retire and is no longer God's hospital, where surgery cuts deep and blood is let and pains are caused and wounds are stitched and prodded and wrapped almost beyond human endurance. God help this church always to remain His hospital whither the Good Samaritan brings us and where we are awakened at the oddest hours and awakened to the most painful realities. Only let them be the realities of God! Only let it all always be pain that is due to His strong pull, ache from Him that cleans out the poison, and wakefulness that may hurt as it will, as long as it wakes us up to God's Easter!

Look at that first Easter again, and see what you can see there, and see whether it is a peaceful idyll that is best heard under the influence of the spring song. The women start out for a tomb, and they weren't expecting a thing except a renewal of their basic heartache and even additional difficulties that they had not thought to provide for. They were on an errand of mercy and love, the same as when you take flowers to the cemetery. You know that there will be no reward in it for you, that the little visit will give you no expression from the one you are visiting but will only open again the old grief which time has begun to heal. These women were on their way to anoint the dead body of Jesus. It was the least that they could do for Him who had done so much for them. Someone surely had to express some love there where there had been nothing but hate. No matter what anyone had said about Him, God could hardly be displeased if they would anoint His body the way all the dead bodies of the Jews were anointed. After all, He also was a son of Abraham, and

115

don't forget it, He had been very good to them while He was alive, just as good as anyone could possibly be. You can take any funeral that you have ever been to, any expression of last respects that you know of, and you have the same thing on the part of these women. You can fill in all the gaps here with your own experiences, because in this area they are all the same. And we are all in this area, and we are all always on our way to the cemetery, only that we are talking about things different from what they talked about. We've got a whole new set of subjects, A-bombs and nuclear war and summit conferences and cancer and heart disease and TV, but it is no more than conversation on the way to the cemetery either to visit the dead or to lie down and die there ourselves. It is really all that you can expect, and the grave of everyone who ever lived is death's proof of our own destiny.

But where were the men, the brave followers of Jesus, the ardent advocates of His cause when He was still alive, the proud confessors of undying loyalty to Him though they should suffer imprisonment and martyrdom for Him? Mind you, this is not a confirmation reunion that we are holding this morning, although the questions would be most fitting. These are questions that we are asking of disciples of another day, and it only goes to show that the questions always fit disciples of all days. Well, for the men the light had gone out, and the glory had departed, and they were left right back where they had started, with their old workaday world that they had thought to escape, with memories of how they had been duped, and with only one certainty — that they would never be taken in that way again. This doesn't sound too unlike modern ex-disciples either, people who learned a lot of stuff when they were kids and then went on to higher learning (that often is a laugh all by itself). And now they know how

116

some pastor lorded it over them and shot them full of nonsense that science has long ago exploded, and now they'd sure like to tell that pastor a thing or two from their exceedingly high vantage point of much higher learning.

And all around in Jerusalem and elsewhere life went on as usual, the ordinary life in which people still slept because it was very early; the pleasurable life in which people needed sleep because of the night before; the lonely life in which people had whole beds and whole rooms and whole houses altogether to themselves; the despairing life where other ropes were being strung up alongside of Judas' girdle and where you could still see on the ground where his bowels had gushed forth; the anxious life where worry has become a habit and where people are more afraid of life than they are of death but where there is always nothing but fear; the materialistic life where the sleep is very sound when the barns and the banks are full, or where the sleep is fitful because its god can be killed, or where there is no sleep at all lest moths and rust should corrupt and thieves break through to steal; the young life that cannot be bothered with God and the things of God, and the old life which spends its time in vain regret that it wasn't more bothered in its long past with God and the things of God; the life of which men say that this surely was the life, and the life in which men curse the day of their birth in order that they might die: all of this was all about the tomb of Jesus that first Easter morning just as surely as it is about us and in us today.

Before Easter can say a word to us, we've got to answer the questions, Where are we? In what classification must we be listed? It is essential to know where you are before you can decide where you want to go.

117

We are there, and we are classified not according to our own opinion of ourselves, not according to the classifications into which other people place us, but we are classified this morning and always in our relation to that tomb where the women were going. We may want nothing to do with it; we may insist that it is irrelevant; we may try to be indifferent; we may say that we are making our pilgrimage to it this morning; we may assert that it has no meaning for this modern world and our individual modern life. But we are what we are in relation to it, and we are doing what we are doing and living the way we are living solely on the basis of what we believe with regard to it. That is what Easter is really all about, and it is all about every man who lives and every man who has ever died, whether a man wants it that way or not, whether a man sees it that way or not. God alone is Judge, and He does not first ask us by what standards we want to be judged. He has already set them, and we are fools if we do not know them, and we are even greater fools if we think to evade them.

If we look closely at the entire Easter event, we notice that we are told nothing about the event itself. We are not taken into the tomb and given a description of just exactly what took place there. All that we have is a "before" and an "after," and the reality of what took place is brought home to us primarily in the tremendous difference between the "before" and the "after." "Before" men had gone to extra pains to keep this Jesus in the grave, always man's vain attempt in shutting God into some little tomb of man's building behind a great stone of man's own rolling. "After" soldiers had to lie, and Jewish leaders had to pay out more money, and Pilate's seal had to be shown as valueless, and cowardly men had to be depicted as brave enough to rob a grave

118

of a corpse that was the final proof of how they had been deceived. "Before" the women had gone sorrowing, and "after" they go running back in sheer panic, so frightened, not overjoyed, mind you, but so frightened that they wouldn't even tell anyone about what they had been commanded by an angel to tell. Now without any boasting "before" and without any fanfare of how radically they had changed, these ex-disciples, these sitters behind locked doors out of fear of the Jews, actually, in the "after," become the brave confessors that they had once boasted to be and died the death of martyrdom, which previously they just could not stomach. What happened? Perhaps we had better be warned, because if it happened to them it could well happen to us — if we come to believe what they come to believe.

Jesus had risen from the dead. The Crucified One was alive again. The unexpected had happened. The last thing that ever entered their mind not only entered their mind now but also laid hold of them as the single reality of life. "Before" and "after"! It brings to mind the comment of St. Paul "If Christ be not raised, then our faith is vain." That is the "before" which we see in the disciples and the women, the "before" in which we, too, largely live. "But now is Christ risen." That is the "after" which alone explains what happened to these people. Is this "after" for us? Or are we doomed to sit in this "before"? Is life nothing but time, the passing of time until all time is past for us? Or are we in the midst of eternity right now, so that living now finds its true meaning in fulfillment, in this that we shall never die? How can we be sure? There are those who will tell you that you cannot be sure unless you can put your finger into the nailprints and thrust your hands into the side that was opened on the cross with

119

the slash of the spear. In a sense that is correct if by being sure we mean to be as certain as we are of the five fingers on our hand. But then there is something else that you must be equally sure of: in that same sense you cannot be sure either that Jesus did not rise again from the dead. Which puts us squarely in a dilemma if we have to be sure in that particular way of being sure. Either way you are going to come up with a faith with regard to Easter, a faith that will determine your living and your dying, a faith that will be altogether decisive for all your days and for your eternity as well.

Can we be sure that Jesus rose from the dead? We can be sure in faith, but only in faith, even though there are any number of evidences that speak strongly in that direction. That means that we can be sure only as the disciples were sure and as the women were sure: on the basis of Christ's own Word. Remember, Jesus is not a shock therapist, and whenever He let Himself be seen by the disciples or the women, there always had to be the interpretation of His Word, the renewal of promises made long before, the granting again of that peace which He had given them before He died. It is that same Word which works the same certainty of faith today, so that the only knowing that there is is in faith and under the Word; the only certainty that there is is the certainty that comes from believing. And there can never be faith if we stand aside and speculate, if we merely look in without giving ourselves, if we only hear what is said but are not willing to surrender to Him who speaks. Anything except faith still seeks the Living One among the dead, anything else is denial because it is the refusal to live life on God's terms and under God's directions. That is not Easter morn but the black night of unbelief, which always ends in despair. That is not being of God, whose Christ lives and is Lord indeed, but it is still being our own god to know good and evil, to know what is true and not true, to know all by ourselves how things surely must be and how they cannot possibly be.

The world is not the same since that first Easter. You are not the same since you first came into contact with God's Easter. Now you are either a believer in God's life in the risen Christ, or you are a disbeliever in God's life, and you ignore the risen Christ in order to have life on your own terms and by your own standards. Then you are of all men most miserable, not only today, as you sit here, but every single day that you still have left. Here is the only way I know that my Redeemer lives. He has spoken His forgiveness upon me, and now I know what it means to be with God as forgiven indeed. He has invited me to come to Him for rest. I come in faith, and I find rest in His resurrection life. He assures me that I can live in Him. I believe, and lo, I truly live in Him. He promises me power from on high, and now I have the power of faith, so that though God slay me, yet I can trust in Him. He has said to me: "Peace be unto you," and now I am at peace with God. He goes before me as He said He would, and I have only to listen to hear Him urge me on again with His call: "Take up your cross, and follow Me." I believe! I cannot help it! I have looked into the empty tomb, and I have heard the angel, and I too have been filled with terror no less because Jesus lives, lives to look into my heart when I worship and into my eyes wherever I look and into my hands whatever I grasp. But the terror is gone now because I believe that it is the Crucified One who lives, the One who died for me, though I cannot feel it. Now there is One walking with me, moment by moment and day by day, giving me the victory, His victory

121

that overcomes the world, even faith. Now whenever I become anxious because life is too much with me and I have altogether too little to meet it with, now I kneel and listen to His great "Fear not," and I have nothing left to do but worship and adore this Jesus, who died for me and rose again, my Lord and my God! Happy Easter! Blessed Easter! Joyous Easter! Look who joins you in your way this morn. Look who walks by your side, always by your side, right where you are. Look again at the scars. It is the Crucified One, who died for you. Now He lives. He lives who once was dead! He lives, my everliving Head! Now, right now, He lives for you. Amen.